RESUMES FOR
NURSING CAREERS

THIRD EDITION

RESUMES FOR

NURSING CAREERS

The Editors of McGraw-Hill

New York Chicago San Francisco Lisbon London Madrid Mexico City
Milan New Delhi San Juan Seoul Singapore Sydney Toronto

The **McGraw·Hill** Companies

Library of Congress Cataloging-in-Publication Data

Resumes for nursing careers / by the editors of McGraw-Hill. — 3rd ed.
  p.   cm.
ISBN 0-07-147620-2 (alk. paper)
1. Nurses—Employment.   2. Resumes (Employment)   3. Nursing—
Vocational guidance.   I. McGraw-Hill Book Company.

RT86.7.R45   2007
650.14'202461—dc22   2006051438

1 2 3 4 5 6 7 8 9 10 11 12 13 14 15 16 17 18 19 20   QPD/QPD   0 9 8 7

ISBN-13: 978-0-07-147620-1
ISBN-10:   0-07-147620-2

McGraw-Hill books are available at special quantity discounts to use as premiums and
sales promotions, or for use in corporate training programs. For more information, please
write to the Director of Special Sales, Professional Publishing, McGraw-Hill, Two Penn
Plaza, New York, NY 10121-2298. Or contact your local bookstore.

This book is printed on acid-free paper.

Contents

Introduction

Your resume is a piece of paper (or an electronic document) that serves to introduce you to the people who will eventually hire you. To write a thoughtful resume, you must thoroughly assess your personality, your accomplishments, and the skills you have acquired. The act of composing and submitting a resume also requires you to carefully consider the company or individual that might hire you. What are they looking for, and how can you meet their needs? This book shows you how to organize your personal information and experience into a concise and well-written resume, so that your qualifications and potential as an employee will be understood easily and quickly by a complete stranger.

Writing the resume is just one step in what can be a daunting job-search process, but it is an important element in the chain of events that will lead you to your new position. While you are probably a talented, bright, and charming person, your resume may not reflect these qualities. A poorly written resume can get you nowhere; a well-written resume can land you an interview and potentially a job. A good resume can even lead the interviewer to ask you questions that will allow you to talk about your strengths and highlight the skills you can bring to a prospective employer. Even a person with very little experience can find a good job if he or she is assisted by a thoughtful and polished resume.

Lengthy, typewritten resumes are a thing of the past. Today, employers do not have the time or the patience for verbose documents; they look for tightly composed, straightforward, action-based resumes. Although a one-page resume is the norm, a two-page resume may be warranted if you have had extensive job experience or have changed careers and truly need the space to properly position yourself. If, after careful editing, you still need more than one page to present yourself, it's acceptable to use a second page. A crowded resume that's hard to read would be the worst of your choices.

Distilling your work experience, education, and interests into such a small space requires preparation and thought. This book takes you step-by-step through the process of crafting an effective resume that will stand out in today's competitive marketplace. It serves as a workbook and a place to write down your experiences, while also including the techniques you'll need to pull all the necessary elements together. In the following pages, you'll find many examples of resumes that are specific to your area of interest. Study them for inspiration and find what appeals to you. There are a variety of ways to organize and present your information; inside, you'll find several that will be suitable to your needs. Good luck landing the job of your dreams!

The Elements of an Effective Resume

An effective resume is composed of information that employers are most interested in knowing about a prospective job applicant. This information is conveyed by a few essential elements. The following is a list of elements that are found in most resumes—some essential, some optional. Later in this chapter, we will further examine the role of each of these elements in the makeup of your resume.

- Heading

- Objective and/or Keyword Section

- Work Experience

- Education

- Honors

- Activities

- Certificates and Licenses

- Publications

- Professional Memberships

- Special Skills

- Personal Information

- References

The first step in preparing your resume is to gather information about yourself and your past accomplishments. Later you will refine this information, rewrite it using effective language, and organize it into an attractive layout. But first, let's take a look at each of these important elements individually so you can judge their appropriateness for your resume.

Heading

Although the heading may seem to be the simplest section of your resume, be careful not to take it lightly. It is the first section your prospective employer will see, and it contains the information she or he will need to contact you. At the very least, the heading must contain your name, your home address, and, of course, a phone number where you can be reached easily.

In today's high-tech world, many of us have multiple ways that we can be contacted. You may list your e-mail address if you are reasonably sure the employer makes use of this form of communication. Keep in mind, however, that others may have access to your e-mail messages if you send them from an account provided by your current company. If this is a concern, do not list your work e-mail address on your resume. If you are able to take calls at your current place of business, you should include your work number, because most employers will attempt to contact you during typical business hours.

If you have voice mail or a reliable answering machine at home or at work, list its number in the heading and make sure your greeting is professional and clear. Always include at least one phone number in your heading, even if it is a temporary number, where a prospective employer can leave a message.

You might have a dozen different ways to be contacted, but you do not need to list all of them. Confine your numbers or addresses to those that are the easiest for the prospective employer to use and the simplest for you to retrieve.

Objective

When seeking a specific career path, it is important to list a job or career objective on your resume. This statement helps employers know the direction you see yourself taking, so they can determine whether your goals are in line with those of their organization and the position available. Normally, an objective is one to two sentences long. Its contents will vary depending on your career field, goals, and personality. The objective can be specific or general, but it should always be to the point. See the sample resumes in this book for examples.

If you are planning to use this resume online, or you suspect your potential employer is likely to scan your resume, you will want to include a "keyword" in the objective. This allows a prospective employer, searching hundreds of resumes for a specific skill or position objective, to locate the keyword and find your resume. In essence, a keyword is what's "hot" in your particular field at a given time. It's a buzzword, a shorthand way of getting a particular message across at a glance. For example, if you are a lawyer, your objective might state your desire to work in the area of corporate litigation. In this case, someone searching for the keyword "corporate litigation" will pull up your resume and know that you want to plan, research, and present cases at trial on behalf of the corporation. If your objective states that you "desire a challenging position in systems design," the keyword is "systems design," an industry-specific shorthand way of saying that you want to be involved in assessing the need for, acquiring, and implementing high-technology systems. These are keywords and every industry has them, so it's becoming more and more important to include a few in your resume. (You may need to conduct additional research to make sure you know what keywords are most likely to be used in your desired industry, profession, or situation.)

There are many resume and job-search sites online. Like most things in the online world, they vary a great deal in quality. Use your discretion. If you plan to apply for jobs online or advertise your availability this way, you will want to design a scannable resume. This type of resume uses a format that can be easily scanned into a computer and added to a database. Scanning allows a prospective employer to use keywords to quickly review each applicant's experience and skills, and (in the event that there are many candidates for the job) to keep your resume for future reference.

Many people find that it is worthwhile to create two or more versions of their basic resume. You may want an intricately designed resume on high-quality paper to mail or hand out *and* a resume that is designed to be scanned into a computer and saved on a database or an online job site. You can even create a resume in ASCII text to e-mail to prospective employers. For further information, you may wish to refer to the *Guide to Internet Job Searching*, by Frances Roehm and Margaret Dikel, updated and published every other year by McGraw-Hill. This excellent book contains helpful and detailed information about formatting a resume for Internet use. To get you started, in Chapter 3 we have included a list of things to keep in mind when creating electronic resumes.

Although it is usually a good idea to include an objective, in some cases this element is not necessary. The goal of the objective statement is to provide the employer with an idea of where you see yourself going in the field. However, if you are uncertain of the exact nature of the job you seek, including an objective that is too specific could result in your not being considered for a host of perfectly acceptable positions. If you decide not to use an objective heading in your resume, you should definitely incorporate the information that would be conveyed in the objective into your cover letter.

Work Experience

Work experience is arguably the most important element of them all. Unless you are a recent graduate or former homemaker with little or no relevant work experience, your current and former positions will provide the central focus of the resume. You will want this section to be as complete and carefully constructed as possible. By thoroughly examining your work experience, you can get to the heart of your accomplishments and present them in a way that demonstrates and highlights your qualifications.

If you are just entering the workforce, your resume will probably focus on your education, but you should also include information on your work or volunteer experiences. Although you will have less information about work experience than a person who has held multiple positions or is advanced in his or her career, the amount of information is not what is most important in this section. How the information is presented and what it says about you as a worker and a person are what really count.

As you create this section of your resume, remember the need for accuracy. Include all the necessary information about each of your jobs, including your job title, dates of employment, name of your employer, city, state, responsibilities, special projects you handled, and accomplishments. Be sure to list only accomplishments for which you were directly responsible. And don't be alarmed if you haven't participated in or worked on special projects, because this section may not be relevant to certain jobs.

The most common way to list your work experience is in *reverse chronological order*. In other words, start with your most recent job and work your way backward. This way, your prospective employer sees your current (and often most important) position before considering your past employment. Your most recent position, if it's the most important in terms of responsibilities and relevance to the job for which you are applying, should also be the one that includes the most information as compared to your previous positions.

Even if the work itself seems unrelated to your proposed career path, you should list any job or experience that will help sell your talents. If you were promoted or given greater responsibilities or commendations, be sure to mention the fact.

The following worksheet is provided to help you organize your experiences in the working world. It will also serve as an excellent resource to refer to when updating your resume in the future.

WORK EXPERIENCE

Job One:

Job Title _____

Dates _____

Employer _____

City, State _____

Major Duties _____

_____

_____

_____

_____

_____

_____

_____

_____

Special Projects _____

_____

_____

_____

Accomplishments _____

_____

_____

_____

_____

_____

Job Two:

Job Title _____

Dates _____

Employer _____

City, State _____

Major Duties _____

_____

_____

_____

_____

_____

_____

_____

Special Projects _____

_____

_____

_____

Accomplishments _____

_____

_____

_____

_____

_____

_____

_____

Job Three:

Job Title _____

Dates _____

Employer _____

City, State _____

Major Duties _____

_____

_____

_____

_____

_____

_____

_____

Special Projects _____

_____

_____

_____

Accomplishments _____

_____

_____

_____

_____

_____

_____

_____

Job Four:

Job Title _____

Dates _____

Employer _____

City, State _____

Major Duties _____

_____

_____

_____

_____

_____

_____

_____

Special Projects _____

_____

_____

_____

Accomplishments _____

_____

_____

_____

_____

_____

_____

_____

Education

Education is usually the second most important element of a resume. Your educational background is often a deciding factor in an employer's decision to interview you. Highlight your accomplishments in school as much as you did those accomplishments at work. If you are looking for your first professional job, your education or life experience will be your greatest asset because your related work experience will be minimal. In this case, the education section becomes the most important means of selling yourself.

Include in this section all the degrees or certificates you have received; your major or area of concentration; all of the honors you earned; and any relevant activities you participated in, organized, or chaired. Again, list your most recent schooling first. If you have completed graduate-level work, begin with that and work your way back through your undergraduate education. If you have completed college, you generally should not list your high-school experience; do so only if you earned special honors, you had a grade point average that was much better than the norm, or this was your highest level of education.

If you have completed a large number of credit hours in a subject that may be relevant to the position you are seeking but did not obtain a degree, you may wish to list the hours or classes you completed. Keep in mind, however, that you may be asked to explain why you did not finish the program. If you are currently in school, list the degree, certificate, or license you expect to obtain and the projected date of completion.

The following worksheet will help you gather the information you need for this section of your resume.

EDUCATION

School One _____

Major or Area of Concentration _____

Degree _____

Dates _____

School Two _____

Major or Area of Concentration _____

Degree _____

Dates _____

Honors

If you include an honors section in your resume, you should highlight any awards, honors, or memberships in honorary societies that you have received. (You may also incorporate this information into your education section.) Often, the honors are academic in nature, but this section also may be used for special achievements in sports, clubs, or other school activities. Always include the name of the organization awarding the honor and the date(s) received. Use the following worksheet to help you gather your information.

HONORS

Honor One _____

Awarding Organization _____

Date(s) _____

Honor Two _____

Awarding Organization _____

Date(s) _____

Honor Three _____

Awarding Organization _____

Date(s) _____

Honor Four _____

Awarding Organization _____

Date(s) _____

Honor Five _____

Awarding Organization _____

Date(s) _____

Activities

Perhaps you have been active in different organizations or clubs; often an employer will look at such involvement as evidence of initiative, dedication, and good social skills. Examples of your ability to take a leading role in a group should be included on a resume, if you can provide them. The activities section of your resume should present neighborhood and community activities, volunteer positions, and so forth. In general, you may want to avoid listing any organization whose name indicates the race, creed, sex, age, marital status, sexual orientation, or nation of origin of its members because this could expose you to discrimination. Use the following worksheet to list the specifics of your activities.

ACTIVITIES

Organization/Activity _____

Accomplishments _____

_____

_____

Organization/Activity _____

Accomplishments _____

_____

_____

Organization/Activity _____

Accomplishments _____

_____

_____

As your work experience grows through the years, your school activities and honors will carry less weight and be emphasized less in your resume. Eventually, you will probably list only your degree and any major honors received. As time goes by, your job performance and the experience you've gained become the most important elements in your resume, which should change to reflect this.

Certificates and Licenses

If your chosen career path requires specialized training, you may already have certificates or licenses. You should list these if the job you are seeking requires them and you, of course, have acquired them. If you have applied for a license but have not yet received it, use the phrase "application pending."

License requirements vary by state. If you have moved or are planning to relocate to another state, check with that state's board or licensing agency for all licensing requirements.

Always make sure that all of the information you list is completely accurate. Locate copies of your certificates and licenses, and check the exact date and name of the accrediting agency. Use the following worksheet to organize the necessary information.

CERTIFICATES AND LICENSES

Name of License _____

Licensing Agency _____

Date Issued _____

Name of License _____

Licensing Agency _____

Date Issued _____

Name of License _____

Licensing Agency _____

Date Issued _____

Publications

Some professions strongly encourage or even require that you publish. If you have written, coauthored, or edited any books, articles, professional papers, or works of a similar nature that pertain to your field, you will definitely want to include this element. Remember to list the date of publication and the publisher's name, and specify whether you were the sole author or a coauthor. Book, magazine, or journal titles are generally italicized, while the titles of articles within a larger publication appear in quotes. (Check with your reference librarian for more about the appropriate way to present this information.) For scientific or research papers, you will need to give the date, place, and audience to whom the paper was presented.

Use the following worksheet to help you gather the necessary information about your publications.

PUBLICATIONS

Title and Type (Note, Article, etc.) _____

Title of Publication (Journal, Book, etc.) _____

Publisher _____

Date Published _____

Title and Type (Note, Article, etc.) _____

Title of Publication (Journal, Book, etc.) _____

Publisher _____

Date Published _____

Title and Type (Note, Article, etc.) _____

Title of Publication (Journal, Book, etc.) _____

Publisher _____

Date Published _____

Professional Memberships

Another potential element in your resume is a section listing professional memberships. Use this section to describe your involvement in professional associations, unions, and similar organizations. It is to your advantage to list any professional memberships that pertain to the job you are seeking. Many employers see your membership as representative of your desire to stay up-to-date and connected in your field. Include the dates of your involvement and whether you took part in any special activities or held any offices within the organization. Use the following worksheet to organize your information.

PROFESSIONAL MEMBERSHIPS

Name of Organization _____

Office(s) Held_____

Activities _____

Dates _____

Name of Organization _____

Office(s) Held_____

Activities _____

Dates _____

Name of Organization _____

Office(s) Held_____

Activities _____

Dates _____

Name of Organization _____

Office(s) Held_____

Activities _____

Dates _____

Special Skills

The special skills section of your resume is the place to mention any special abilities you have that relate to the job you are seeking. You can use this element to present certain talents or experiences that are not necessarily a part of your education or work experience. Common examples include fluency in a foreign language, extensive travel abroad, or knowledge of a particular computer application. "Special skills" can encompass a wide range of talents, and this section can be used creatively. However, for each skill you list, you should be able to describe how it would be a direct asset in the type of work you're seeking because employers may ask just that in an interview. If you can't think of a way to do this, it may be extraneous information.

Personal Information

Some people include personal information on their resumes. This is generally not recommended, but you might wish to include it if you think that something in your personal life, such as a hobby or talent, has some bearing on the position you are seeking. This type of information is often referred to at the beginning of an interview, when it may be used as an icebreaker. Of course, personal information regarding your age, marital status, race, religion, or sexual orientation should never appear on your resume as personal information. It should be given only in the context of memberships and activities, and only when doing so would not expose you to discrimination.

References

References are not usually given on the resume itself, but a prospective employer needs to know that you have references who may be contacted if necessary. All you need to include is a single sentence at the end of the resume: "References are available upon request," or even simply, "References available." Have a reference list ready—your interviewer may ask to see it! Contact each person on the list ahead of time to see whether it is all right for you to use him or her as a reference. This way, the person has a chance to think about what to say *before* the call occurs. This helps ensure that you will obtain the best reference possible.

Chapter 2

Writing Your Resume

Now that you have gathered the information for each section of your resume, it's time to write it out in a way that will get the attention of the reviewer—hopefully, your future employer! The language you use in your resume will affect its success, so you must be careful and conscientious. Translate the facts you have gathered into the active, precise language of resume writing. You will be aiming for a resume that keeps the reader's interest and highlights your accomplishments in a concise and effective way.

Resume writing is unlike any other form of writing. Although your seventh-grade composition teacher would not approve, the rules of punctuation and sentence building are often completely ignored. Instead, you should try for a functional, direct writing style that focuses on the use of verbs and other words that imply action on your part. Writing with action words and strong verbs characterizes you to potential employers as an energetic, active person, someone who completes tasks and achieves results from his or her work. Resumes that do not make use of action words can sound passive and stale. These resumes are not effective and do not get the attention of any employer, no matter how qualified the applicant. Choose words that display your strengths and demonstrate your initiative. The following list of commonly used verbs will help you create a strong resume:

administered	assembled
advised	assumed responsibility
analyzed	billed
arranged	built

carried out

channeled

collected

communicated

compiled

completed

conducted

contacted

contracted

coordinated

counseled

created

cut

designed

determined

developed

directed

dispatched

distributed

documented

edited

established

expanded

functioned as

gathered

handled

hired

implemented

improved

inspected

interviewed

introduced

invented

maintained

managed

met with

motivated

negotiated

operated

orchestrated

ordered

organized

oversaw

performed

planned

prepared

presented

produced

programmed

published

purchased

recommended

recorded

reduced

referred

represented

researched

reviewed

saved	supervised
screened	taught
served as	tested
served on	trained
sold	typed
suggested	wrote

Let's look at two examples that differ only in their writing style. The first resume section is ineffective because it does not use action words to accent the applicant's work experiences.

WORK EXPERIENCE
Regional Sales Manager

Manager of sales representatives from seven states. Manager of twelve food chain accounts in the East. In charge of the sales force's planned selling toward specific goals. Supervisor and trainer of new sales representatives. Consulting for customers in the areas of inventory management and quality control.

Special Projects: Coordinator and sponsor of annual Food Industry Seminar.

Accomplishments: Monthly regional volume went up 25 percent during my tenure while, at the same time, a proper sales/cost ratio was maintained. Customer-company relations were improved.

In the following paragraph, we have rewritten the same section using action words. Notice how the tone has changed. It now sounds stronger and more active. This person accomplished goals and really *did* things.

WORK EXPERIENCE
Regional Sales Manager

Managed sales representatives from seven states. Oversaw twelve food chain accounts in the eastern United States. Directed the sales force in planned selling toward specific goals. Supervised and trained new sales representatives. Counseled customers in the areas of inventory management and quality control. Coordinated and sponsored the annual Food Industry Seminar. Increased monthly regional volume by 25 percent and helped to improve customer-company relations during my tenure.

One helpful way to construct the work experience section is to make use of your actual job descriptions—the written duties and expectations your employers have for a person in your current or former position. Job descriptions are rarely written in proper resume language, so you will have to rework them, but they do include much of the information necessary to create this section of your resume. If you have access to job descriptions for your former positions, you can use the details to construct an action-oriented paragraph. Often, your human resources department can provide a job description for your current position.

The following is an example of a typical human resources job description, followed by a rewritten version of the same description employing action words and specific details about the job. Again, pay attention to the style of writing instead of the content, as the details of your own experience will be unique.

WORK EXPERIENCE
Public Administrator I

Responsibilities: Coordinate and direct public services to meet the needs of the nation, state, or community. Analyze problems; work with special committees and public agencies; recommend solutions to governing bodies.

Aptitudes and Skills: Ability to relate to and communicate with people; solve complex problems through analysis; plan, organize, and implement policies and programs. Knowledge of political systems, financial management, personnel administration, program evaluation, and organizational theory.

WORK EXPERIENCE
Public Administrator I

Wrote pamphlets and conducted discussion groups to inform citizens of legislative processes and consumer issues. Organized and supervised 25 interviewers. Trained interviewers in effective communication skills.

After you have written out your resume, you are ready to begin the next important step: assembly and layout.

Chapter 3

Assembly and Layout

At this point, you've gathered all the necessary information for your resume and rewritten it in language that will impress your potential employers. Your next step is to assemble the sections in a logical order and lay them out on the page neatly and attractively to achieve the desired effect: getting the interview.

Assembly

The order of the elements in a resume makes a difference in its overall effect. Clearly, you would not want to bury your name and address somewhere in the middle of the resume. Nor would you want to lead with a less important section, such as special skills. Put the elements in an order that stresses your most important accomplishments and the things that will be most appealing to your potential employer. For example, if you are new to the workforce, you will want the reviewer to read about your education and life skills before any part-time jobs you may have held for short durations. On the other hand, if you have been gainfully employed for several years and currently hold an important position in your company, you should list your work accomplishments ahead of your educational information, which has become less pertinent with time.

Certain things should always be included in your resume, but others are optional. The following list shows you which are which. You might want to use it as a checklist to be certain that you have included all of the necessary information.

Essential	**Optional**
Name	Cellular Phone Number
Address	Pager Number
Phone Number	E-Mail Address or Website Address
Work Experience	Voice Mail Number
Education	Job Objective
References Phrase	Honors
	Special Skills
	Publications
	Professional Memberships
	Activities
	Certificates and Licenses
	Personal Information
	Graphics
	Photograph

Your choice of optional sections depends on your own background and employment needs. Always use information that will put you in a favorable light—unless it's absolutely essential, avoid anything that will prompt the interviewer to ask questions about your weaknesses or something else that could be unflattering. Make sure your information is accurate and truthful. If your honors are impressive, include them in the resume. If your activities in school demonstrate talents that are necessary for the job you are seeking, allow space for a section on activities. If you are applying for a position that requires ornamental illustration, you may want to include border illustrations or graphics that demonstrate your talents in this area. If you are answering an advertisement for a job that requires certain physical traits, a photo of yourself might be appropriate. A person applying for a job as a computer programmer would *not* include a photo as part of his or her resume. Each resume is unique, just as each person is unique.

Types of Resumes

So far we have focused on the most common type of resume—the *reverse chronological* resume—in which your most recent job is listed first. This is the type of resume usually preferred by those who have to read a large number of resumes, and it is by far the most popular and widely circulated. However, this style of presentation may not be the most effective way to highlight *your* skills and accomplishments.

For example, if you are reentering the workforce after many years or are trying to change career fields, the *functional* resume may work best. This type of resume puts the focus on your achievements instead of the sequence of your work history. In the functional resume, your experience is presented through your general accomplishments and the skills you have developed in your working life.

A functional resume is assembled from the same information you gathered in Chapter 1. The main difference lies in how you organize the information. Essentially, the work experience section is divided in two, with your job duties and accomplishments constituting one section and your employers' names, cities, and states; your positions; and the dates employed making up the other. Place the first section near the top of your resume, just below your job objective (if used), and call it *Accomplishments* or *Achievements*. The second section, containing the bare essentials of your work history, should come after the accomplishments section and can be called *Employment History*, since it is a chronological overview of your former jobs.

The other sections of your resume remain the same. The work experience section is the only one affected in the functional format. By placing the section that focuses on your achievements at the beginning, you draw attention to these achievements. This puts less emphasis on where you worked and when, and more on what you did and what you are capable of doing.

If you are changing careers, the emphasis on skills and achievements is important. The identities of previous employers (who aren't part of your new career field) need to be downplayed. A functional resume can help accomplish this task. If you are reentering the workforce after a long absence, a functional resume is the obvious choice. And if you lack full-time work experience, you will need to draw attention away from this fact and put the focus on your skills and abilities. You may need to highlight your volunteer activities and part-time work. Education may also play a more important role in your resume.

The type of resume that is right for you will depend on your personal circumstances. It may be helpful to create both types and then compare them. Which one presents you in the best light? Examples of both types of resumes are included in this book. Use the sample resumes in Chapter 5 to help you decide on the content, presentation, and look of your own resume.

Resume or Curriculum Vitae?

A curriculum vitae (CV) is a longer, more detailed synopsis of your professional history that generally runs three or more pages in length. It includes a summary of your educational and academic background as well as teaching and research experience, publications, presentations, awards, honors, affiliations, and other details. Because the purpose of the CV is different from that of the resume, many of the rules we've discussed thus far involving style and length do not apply.

A curriculum vitae is used primarily for admissions applications to graduate or professional schools, independent consulting in a variety of settings, proposals for fellowships or grants, or applications for positions in academia. As with a resume, you may need different versions of a CV for different types of positions. You should only send a CV when one is specifically requested by an employer or institution.

Like a resume, your CV should include your name, contact information, education, skills, and experience. In addition to the basics, a CV includes research and teaching experience, publications, grants and fellowships, professional associations and licenses, awards, and other information relevant to the position for which you are applying. You can follow the advice presented thus far to gather and organize your personal information.

Special Tips for Electronic Resumes

Because there are many details to consider in writing a resume that will be posted or transmitted on the Internet, or one that will be scanned into a computer when it is received, we suggest that you refer to the *Guide to Internet Job Searching*, by Frances Roehm and Margaret Dikel, as previously mentioned. However, here are some brief, general guidelines to follow if you expect your resume to be scanned into a computer.

- Use standard fonts in which none of the letters touch.

- Keep in mind that underlining, italics, and fancy scripts may not scan well.

- Use boldface and capitalization to set off elements. Again, make sure letters don't touch. Leave at least a quarter inch between lines of type.

- Keep information and elements at the left margin. Centering, columns, and even indenting may change when the resume is optically scanned.

- Do not use any lines, boxes, or graphics.

- Place the most important information at the top of the first page. If you use two pages, put "Page 1 of 2" at the bottom of the first page and put your name and "Page 2 of 2" at the top of the second page.

- List each telephone number on its own line in the header.

- Use multiple keywords or synonyms for what you do to make sure your qualifications will be picked up if a prospective employer is searching for them. Use nouns that are keywords for your profession.

- Be descriptive in your titles. For example, don't just use "assistant"; use "legal office assistant."

- Make sure the contrast between print and paper is good. Use a high-quality laser printer and white or very light colored 8½-by-11-inch paper.

- Mail a high-quality laser print or an excellent copy. Do not fold or use staples, as this might interfere with scanning. You may, however, use paper clips.

In addition to creating a resume that works well for scanning, you may want to have a resume that can be e-mailed to reviewers. Because you may not know what word processing application the recipient uses, the best format to use is ASCII text. (ASCII stands for "American Standard Code for Information Interchange.") It allows people with very different software platforms to exchange and understand information. (E-mail operates on this principle.) ASCII is a simple, text-only language, which means you can include only simple text. There can be no use of boldface, italics, or even paragraph indentations.

To create an ASCII resume, just use your normal word processing program; when finished, save it as a "text only" document. You will find this option under the "save" or "save as" command. Here is a list of things to *avoid* when crafting your electronic resume:

- Tabs. Use your space bar. Tabs will not work.

- Any special characters, such as mathematical symbols.

- Word wrap. Use hard returns (the return key) to make line breaks.

- Centering or other formatting. Align everything at the left margin.

- Bold or italic fonts. Everything will be converted to plain text when you save the file as a "text only" document.

Check carefully for any mistakes before you save the document as a text file. Spellcheck and proofread it several times; then ask someone with a keen eye to go over it again for you. Remember: the key is to keep it simple. Any attempt to make this resume pretty or decorative may result in a resume that is confusing and hard to read. After you have saved the document, you can cut and paste it into an e-mail or onto a website.

Layout for a Paper Resume

A great deal of care—and much more formatting—is necessary to achieve an attractive layout for your paper resume. There is no single appropriate layout that applies to every resume, but there are a few basic rules to follow in putting your resume on paper:

- Leave a comfortable margin on the sides, top, and bottom of the page (usually one to one and a half inches).

- Use appropriate spacing between the sections (two to three line spaces are usually adequate).

- Be consistent in the *type* of headings you use for different sections of your resume. For example, if you capitalize the heading EMPLOYMENT HISTORY, don't use initial capitals and underlining for a section of equal importance, such as Education.

- Do not use more than one font in your resume. Stay consistent by choosing a font that is fairly standard and easy to read, and don't change it for different sections. Beware of the tendency to try to make your resume original by choosing fancy type styles; your resume may end up looking unprofessional instead of creative. Unless you are in a very creative and artistic field, you should almost always stick with tried-and-true type styles like Times New Roman and Palatino, which are often used in business writing. In the area of resume styles, conservative is usually the best way to go.

CHRONOLOGICAL RESUME

Jill Henderson 1275 Hadfield Road • Jackson, MS 80216 • Pager: (803) 555-8300
Home: (803) 555-2771 • E-mail: jhender@xxx.com

Background
• More than 10 years of experience in public health nursing
• Committed to patient advocacy and social reform
• Experienced, effective mental health counselor

Employment
2001 - Present
Mental Health Counselor • Center Clinic, Jackson, MS
Counsel adolescent and adult women in one-on-one and group settings. Provide a safe and therapeutic environment for women confronting depression, low self-esteem, domestic violence, substance abuse, and other mental health issues. Chart patient progress daily and weekly. Develop long- and short-term therapeutic goals. Provide referral to other agencies and services as necessary. Serve on clinic board of directors.

1999 - 2001
Assistant Director • New Hope Women's Shelter, Ottawa, MS
Assisted director with all aspects of clinic management from fund-raising and long-term planning to daily operation of clinic. Recruited and trained volunteers, managed 24-hour telephone hotline, and assisted with counseling of residents. Admitted new residents and assessed their physical and mental state. Helped design and staff on-site child care program.

1997 - 1999
Public Health Nurse • Ottawa County, Ottawa, MS
Treated patients on-site and at two clinic locations. Assisted patients with home health needs: arranging for equipment, home health aides, or application for residential care. Diverse patient population and wide range of patient needs provided experience in everything from early childhood immunizations to hospice care.

Education
Augustana School of Nursing, RN 1997
University of Washington, B.A. 1993 • Double major in Psychology and Sociology

Credentials
• Mississippi RN license 856-121341
• CPR certification
• Member, American Nurses Association

References Available

FUNCTIONAL RESUME

Lucy Wang

2411 Keystone Road
Madison, Wisconsin 53716
lucywang@xxx.com
Cellular: (608) 555-3445

Objective

RN position as a labor and delivery or postpartum care nurse.

Skills

• Assess and triage patients, both uncomplicated and high-risk deliveries

• Educate patients on pain management techniques during labor, postpartum care, and newborn care

• Assist physicians with deliveries

• Skilled lactation consultant

• Perform primary nursing duties in newborn nursery

• Create comprehensive discharge plans

Credentials

B.S.N., University of Wisconsin, 2001
Wisconsin Nursing License #86410
Labor and Delivery Nurse Specialist, 2004
Member, Association of Women's Health, Obstetric, and Neonatal Nursing

Employers

Madison Hospital
Madison, Wisconsin
Staff Nurse, Labor and Delivery
June 2003 - Present

Women's Health Cooperative
Madison, Wisconsin
Staff Nurse
July 2001 - June 2003

References

Personal and professional references on request

- Always try to fit your resume on one page. If you are having trouble with this, you may be trying to say too much. Edit out any repetitive or unnecessary information, and shorten descriptions of earlier jobs where possible. Ask a friend you trust for feedback on what seems unnecessary or unimportant. For example, you may have included too many optional sections. Today, with the prevalence of the personal computer as a tool, there is no excuse for a poorly laid out resume. Experiment with variations until you are pleased with the result.

Remember that a resume is not an autobiography. Too much information will only get in the way. The more compact your resume, the easier it will be to review. If a person who is swamped with resumes looks at yours, catches the main points, and then calls you for an interview to fill in some of the details, your resume has already accomplished its task. A clear and concise resume makes for a happy reader and a good impression.

There are times when, despite extensive editing, the resume simply cannot fit on one page. In this case, the resume should be laid out on two pages in such a way that neither clarity nor appearance is compromised. Each page of a two-page resume should be marked clearly: the first should indicate "Page 1 of 2," and the second should include your name and the page number, for example, "Julia Ramirez—Page 2 of 2." The pages should then be paper-clipped together. You may use a smaller type size (in the same font as the body of your resume) for the page numbers. Place them at the bottom of page one and the top of page two. Again, spend the time now to experiment with the layout until you find one that looks good to you.

Always show your final layout to other people and ask them what they like or dislike about it, and what impresses them most when they read your resume. Make sure that their responses are the same as what you want to elicit from your prospective employer. If they aren't the same, you should continue to make changes until the necessary information is emphasized.

Proofreading

After you have finished typing the master copy of your resume and before you have it copied or printed, thoroughly check it for typing and spelling errors. Do not place all your trust in your computer's spellcheck function. Use an old editing trick and read the whole resume backward—start at the end and read it right to left and bottom to top. This can help you see the small errors or inconsistencies that are easy to overlook. Take time to do it right because a single error on a document this important can cause the reader to judge your attention to detail in a harsh light.

Have several people look at the finished resume just in case you've missed an error. Don't try to take a shortcut; not having an unbiased set of eyes examine your resume now could mean embarrassment later. Even experienced editors can easily overlook their own errors. Be thorough and conscientious with your proofreading so your first impression is a perfect one.

We have included the following rules of capitalization and punctuation to assist you in the final stage of creating your resume. Remember that resumes often require use of a shorthand style of writing that may include sentences without periods and other stylistic choices that break the standard rules of grammar. Be consistent in each section and throughout the whole resume with your choices.

RULES OF CAPITALIZATION

- Capitalize proper nouns, such as names of schools, colleges, and universities; names of companies; and brand names of products.

- Capitalize major words in the names and titles of books, tests, and articles that appear in the body of your resume.

- Capitalize words in major section headings of your resume.

- Do not capitalize words just because they seem important.

- When in doubt, consult a style manual such as *Words into Type* (Prentice Hall) or *The Chicago Manual of Style* (The University of Chicago Press). Your local library can help you locate these and other reference books. Many computer programs also have grammar help sections.

RULES OF PUNCTUATION

- Use commas to separate words in a series.

- Use a semicolon to separate series of words that already include commas within the series. (For an example, see the first rule of capitalization.)

- Use a semicolon to separate independent clauses that are not joined by a conjunction.

- Use a period to end a sentence.

- Use a colon to show that examples or details follow that will expand or amplify the preceding phrase.

- Avoid the use of dashes.

- Avoid the use of brackets.

- If you use any punctuation in an unusual way in your resume, be consistent in its use.

- Whenever you are uncertain, consult a style manual.

Putting Your Resume in Print

You will need to buy high-quality paper for your printer before you print your finished resume. Regular office paper is not good enough for resumes; the reviewer will probably think it looks flimsy and cheap. Go to an office supply store or copy shop and select a high-quality bond paper that will make a good first impression. Select colors like white, off-white, or possibly a light gray. In some industries, a pastel may be acceptable, but be sure the color and feel of the paper make a subtle, positive statement about you. Nothing in the choice of paper should be loud or unprofessional.

If your computer printer does not reproduce your resume properly and produces smudged or stuttered type, either ask to borrow a friend's or take your disk (or a clean original) to a printer or copy shop for high-quality copying. If you anticipate needing a large number of copies, taking your resume to a copy shop or a printer is probably the best choice.

Hold a sheet of your unprinted bond paper up to the light. If it has a watermark, you will want to point this out to the person helping you with copies; the printing should be done so that the reader can read the print and see the watermark the right way up. Check each copy for smudges or streaks. This is the time to be a perfectionist—the results of your careful preparation will be well worth it.

Chapter 4

The Cover Letter

O nce your resume has been assembled, laid out, and printed to
your satisfaction, the next and final step before distribution is to
write your cover letter. Though there may be instances where you
deliver your resume in person, you will usually send it through the mail
or online. Resumes sent through the mail always need an accompanying
letter that briefly introduces you and your resume. The purpose of the cover
letter is to get a potential employer to read your resume, just as the purpose of the resume is to get that same potential employer to call you for
an interview.

   Like your resume, your cover letter should be clean, neat, and direct.
A cover letter usually includes the following information:

1. Your name and address (unless it already appears on your personal
   letterhead) and your phone number(s); see item 7.

2. The date.

3. The name and address of the person and company to whom you
   are sending your resume.

4. The salutation ("Dear Mr." or "Dear Ms." followed by the person's
   last name, or "To Whom It May Concern" if you are answering a
   blind ad).

5. An opening paragraph explaining why you are writing (for example, in response to an ad, as a follow-up to a previous meeting, at
   the suggestion of someone you both know) and indicating that you
   are interested in whatever job is being offered.

6. One or more paragraphs that tell why you want to work for the
   company and what qualifications and experiences you can bring
   to the position. This is a good place to mention some detail about

that particular company that makes you want to work for them; this shows that you have done some research before applying.

7. A final paragraph that closes the letter and invites the reviewer to contact you for an interview. This can be a good place to tell the potential employer which method would be best to use when contacting you. Be sure to give the correct phone number and a good time to reach you, if that is important. You may mention here that your references are available upon request.

8. The closing ("Sincerely" or "Yours truly") followed by your signature in a dark ink, with your name typed under it.

Your cover letter should include all of this information and be no longer than one page in length. The language used should be polite, businesslike, and to the point. Don't attempt to tell your life story in the cover letter; a long and cluttered letter will serve only to annoy the reader. Remember that you need to mention only a few of your accomplishments and skills in the cover letter. The rest of your information is available in your resume. If your cover letter is a success, your resume will be read and all pertinent information reviewed by your prospective employer.

Producing the Cover Letter

Cover letters should always be individualized because they are always written to specific individuals and companies. Never use a form letter for your cover letter or copy it as you would a resume. Each cover letter should be unique, and as personal and lively as possible. (Of course, once you have written and rewritten your first cover letter until you are satisfied with it, you can certainly use similar wording in subsequent letters. You may want to save a template on your computer for future reference.) Keep a hard copy of each cover letter so you know exactly what you wrote in each one.

There are sample cover letters in Chapter 6. Use them as models or for ideas of how to assemble and lay out your own cover letters. Remember that every letter is unique and depends on the particular circumstances of the individual writing it and the job for which he or she is applying.

After you have written your cover letter, proofread it as thoroughly as you did your resume. Again, spelling or punctuation errors are a sure sign of carelessness, and you don't want that to be a part of your first impression on a prospective employer. This is no time to trust your spellcheck function. Even after going through a spelling and grammar check, your cover letter should be carefully proofread by at least one other person.

Print the cover letter on the same quality bond paper you used for your resume. Remember to sign it, using a good dark-ink pen. Handle the letter and resume carefully to avoid smudging or wrinkling, and mail them together in an appropriately sized envelope. Many stores sell matching envelopes to coordinate with your choice of bond paper.

Keep an accurate record of all resumes you send out and the results of each mailing. This record can be kept on your computer, in a calendar or notebook, or on file cards. Knowing when a resume is likely to have been received will keep you on track as you make follow-up phone calls.

About a week after mailing resumes and cover letters to potential employers, contact them by telephone. Confirm that your resume arrived and ask whether an interview might be possible. Be sure to record the name of the person you spoke to and any other information you gleaned from the conversation. It is wise to treat the person answering the phone with a great deal of respect; sometimes the assistant or receptionist has the ear of the person doing the hiring.

You should make a great impression with the strong, straightforward resume and personalized cover letter you have just created. We wish you every success in securing the career of your dreams!

Chapter 5

Sample Resumes

This chapter contains dozens of sample resumes for people pursuing a wide variety of jobs and careers in nursing.

There are many different styles of resumes in terms of graphic layout and presentation of information. These samples represent people with varying amounts of education and experience. Use them as models for your own resume. Choose one resume or borrow elements from several different resumes to help you construct your own.

KEVIN SNYDER

439 Washington Street
Charleston, South Carolina 29425
Home: 803-555-4671
Cell: 803-555-7556

Background

Nearly a decade of nursing experience in hospital ICU and medical/surgical units.
B.S.N. plus critical care certifications. Volunteer and leadership experience.

Skills

- Adept at working with highly sophisticated life support and monitoring equipment.

- Flexible in handling increasingly complex new technologies and treatments in a
fast-paced environment.

- Provide high-quality primary patient care, including IV therapy, monitoring of vital
signs, postoperative wound care, and pain management.

- Delegation to and supervision of nursing assistants, orientation of new staff, and
monitoring of nursing students while providing constructive criticism and soliciting
feedback.

- Active in team-building through extensive voluntary participation in hospital's
community-based health care programs, including blood drives, mobile immunization
efforts, and public speaking engagements.

Employers

Charleston Medical Center
Level II Staff Nurse
2/2004 to Present

St. Mary's Hospital
Per Diem Nurse
2/1999 to 2/2003

Education

B.S.N., South Carolina State College, 1999
- Graduated with Honors
- Sigma Theta Tau, National Honor Society

Certifications: CCRN, PCCN

References available.

CHRISTOPHER WILEY

862 Oak Street
Santa Clara, CA 95051
Home (408) 555-3948
E-mail: cwiley@xxx.com

Goal: Full-time pediatric nursing position at an institution that puts nursing theory into practice to provide high-quality, evidence-based care.

Background: Eight years of hospital nursing experience serving pediatric and geriatric patient populations and their families. Direct patient care from assessment through discharge planning. Practice Comfort Theory, which benefits patients, families, and institutions. Teach health promotion skills and techniques for handling acute health crises to parents. Excellent peer reviews. Wound care and sleep club committee member.

Employers:

Santa Clara Community Hospital	1/2002 - Present
Pediatric Staff Nurse	
St. Andrew's Hospital for Children	2/1999 - 1/2002
Pediatric Staff Nurse	
Quality Home Health Inc.	6/1996 - 2/1999
Case Manager	

Credentials: B.S.N., San Diego State, 1996
California Nursing License 843682
Pediatric Advanced Life Support Certification
CPR Certification
Member, American Nurses Association

Computer Skills: Adept at using new technologies, including computerized charting. Proficient in using Internet medical search engines, including PubMed and Medline.

References: Available with letters of commendation.

MARY L. MURRAY

2155 North Sheffield #2 • Chicago, IL 60614
773.555.0829 • marymurray2@xxx.com

SUMMARY

Highly motivated, dependable nursing graduate seeking a challenging position as an emergency room nurse. Proven ability to initiate appropriate action, follow instructions, and carry out tasks in an efficient manner with experience in patient care, medical management, coordination, and emergency room techniques. Team player with effective interpersonal communication skills and a positive attitude. BLS certified.

EDUCATION

Masters of Science in Nursing, DePaul University - Chicago, IL, anticipated graduation: November 2008
• GPA 3.8/4.0 - Sigma Theta Tau - Nursing Honor Society

Bachelor of Science in Marketing, DePaul University - Chicago, IL, June 2005
• Who's Who Among Students in American Universities and Colleges 2003

CLINICAL EXPERIENCE

Illinois Masonic Hospital (160 hours): Emergency Room
• Worked under the supervision of an RN providing bedside care, treatment, and clinical documentation for adults and pediatrics.
• Handled medication administration, dressing changes, IVs, and all other aspects of nursing care.
• Actively participated with interdisciplinary teams in the development and implementation of individual treatment plans with a broad range of medical/mental health issues.
• Educated patients for home care and discharge planning.

Saint Joseph Hospital: Labor & Delivery

Children's Memorial Hospital: Pediatric Step Down

CLINICAL EXPERIENCE (continued)

Northwestern Memorial Hospital: Cardiac Critical Care, Telemetry, Cardiovascular Thoracic, Intensive Care

Community Health Centers of Chicago: Community Psych

Weiss Memorial Hospital: Orthopedics

St. Joseph's Hospital: General Medicine

PROFESSIONAL EXPERIENCE

NORTHWESTERN MEMORIAL HOSPITAL, Chicago, IL
06/06 - Present
Nursing Assistant
- Responsible for 10-15 patients in the provision of patient care in Neurology/Med-Surgical unit.
- Obtain vital signs and follow up with timely and accurate medical records-keeping procedures.
- Observe and report changes in patients' conditions and other matters of concern.
- Ensure proper use of equipment and medical devices such as wheelchairs, braces, and splinters.
- Assist patients with personal hygiene, grooming, meals, and other needs requiring immediate attention.
- Maintain sanitary, neatness, and safety conditions of rooms in compliance with mandatory regulations.

PLANNED PARENTHOOD, Chicago, IL
09/03 - Present
Volunteer
- Educate and distribute contraceptives to clients of women's health clinic.
- Counsel clients in areas of birth control, emergency contraceptives, and other related issues.

REFERENCES

Available on request.

BRUCE ZAMPIERI

3160 MacGregor Drive
Jefferson City, Missouri 55180
(521) 555-1701
brucezampieri@xxx.com

GOAL

A challenging pediatric nursing position with room for advancement.

BACKGROUND

- Nearly a decade of experience in pediatric nursing, including neonatal intensive care and cardiac care responsibilities.
- Strong commitment to professional development, including design and presentation of in-service workshops, active involvement in Pediatric Nurses Association, and ongoing research on pediatric emergency issues.
- Prompt, accurate, and thorough patient assessments and holistic approach to patient care.
- Practitioner of Virginia Henderson's nursing theory.
- Author of "Nursing Patients to Wellness: Practicing Virginia Henderson's Theory in the Pediatric Setting" (2004, Pediatric Nursing Journal).

EMPLOYMENT HISTORY

Lexington Children's Hospital
St. Louis, Missouri
Level II Pediatric Nurse
March 2005 to Present
Provide direct patient care in 20-bed neonatal ICU at Level One trauma center.
- Triage, assess, and stabilize patients.
- Conduct neurological assessments.
- Monitor and chart patients' progress, dispense medication, and provide IV therapy.

Page 1 of 2

EMPLOYMENT HISTORY (continued)

St. Mary's Medical Center
St. Louis, Missouri
Level II Pediatric Nurse
August 2002 to March 2005
- Pediatric oncology nurse on 15-bed unit.
- Provided chemotherapy treatments.
- Educated and supported patients' families.
- Interacted extensively with radiology and respiratory therapy staff.

Union Hospital
Carson City, Missouri
Level II Pediatric Nurse
January 2000 to August 2002
- Acquired wide range of pediatric experience on 15-bed overflow unit.

EDUCATION

Bachelor's of Nursing
Boston College, School of Nursing
Chestnut Hill, Massachusetts
December 1999
- Graduated with Honors
- Awarded the Selma P. Harding Scholarship, 1997-1999

VOLUNTEER EXPERIENCE

The Night Angels
Jefferson City, Missouri
December 1999 to present
- Provide free health care to Jefferson City's homeless and indigent
  populations in a mobile health care unit.

St. Mary's Hospital, Jolly Trolley
Chestnut Hill, Massachusetts
September 1997 to December 1999
- Delivered ice cream and treats to pediatric oncology patients.

References Available Upon Request

Jill Henderson

1275 Hadfield Road
Jackson, MS 80216
Pager: (803) 555-8300
Home: (803) 555-2771
E-mail: jhender@xxx.com

Background

- More than 10 years of experience in public health nursing
- Committed to patient advocacy and social reform
- Experienced, effective mental health counselor

Employment

2001 - Present • Mental Health Counselor
Center Clinic, Jackson, MS

Counsel adolescent and adult women in one-on-one and group
settings. Provide a safe and therapeutic environment for women
confronting depression, low self-esteem, domestic violence,
substance abuse, and other mental health issues. Chart patient
progress daily and weekly. Develop long- and short-term
therapeutic goals. Provide referral to other agencies and
services as necessary. Serve on clinic board of directors.

1999 - 2001 • Assistant Director
New Hope Women's Shelter, Ottawa, MS

Assisted director with all aspects of clinic management from
fund-raising and long-term planning to daily operation of clinic.
Recruited and trained volunteers, managed 24-hour telephone

Employment (continued)

hotline, and assisted with counseling of residents. Admitted new residents and assessed their physical and mental state. Helped design and staff on-site child care program.

1997 - 1999 • Public Health Nurse
Ottawa County, Ottawa, MS

Treated patients on-site and at two clinic locations. Assisted patients with home health needs: arranging for equipment, home health aides, or application for residential care. Diverse patient population and wide range of patient needs provided experience in everything from early childhood immunizations to hospice care.

Education

Augustana School of Nursing, RN 1997
University of Washington, B.A. 1993, double major in Psychology and Sociology

Credentials

- Mississippi RN license 856-121341
- CPR certification
- Member, American Nurses Association

References Available

Carolyn Meggett, RN

2140 Howe Street
Weston, MA 02193
Cellular: (831) 555-4653

Goal

To use my years of experience in a management position in an emergency room setting.

Experience

4/05 to Present
ER Charge Nurse
Valley View Hospital—Weston, MA

- Coordinate all patient care activities. Work with ER attending physicians to organize systematic flow of patients, expedite delays, and provide optimal care for patients and efficient use of nursing staff.
- Maintain communication and positive rapport with patients, families, and other hospital departments.
- Handle MICU telemetry calls, poison control calls, and medical advice calls.
- Maintain adequate staffing, handle sick calls, and coordinate resource response team coverage for cardiac and multiple trauma patients.
- Maintain adequate inventory of supplies; order or secure additional supplies as needed.

Page 1 of 2

Experience (continued)

3/00 to 4/05
ER Triage Nurse
Wyeth Hospital—Boston, MA

- Assisted charge nurse in maintaining flow of patients and providing appropriate, timely care.
- Communicated patient status and admission or discharge plans to patient and/or family.
- Obtained patient histories and documented patient status and physicians.
- Initiated treatment, providing first aid, ordering X-rays, etc.
- Maintained communication with charge nurse, support staff, patients, and families.
- Notified police on reportable cases.
- Restocked triage supplies.
- Assisted with telemetry calls as needed.

Credentials

RN, Wyeth School of Nursing, Beacon Crest, MA, 2000
TNS (Trauma Nurse Specialist), 2001
CEN (Certified Emergency Nurse), 2000
State of MA Nursing License #615-147782

References

Personal and professional references available and forwarded on request.

Ellen K. Strabinski

283 Stapen Street

Atlanta, Georgia 30301

(404) 555-4494

ellenkstrab@xxx.com

SUMMARY

- B.S.N. with six years of full-time hospital nursing experience

- M.S.N. in progress

- Seeking challenging nursing position with opportunity to acquire supervisory skills

EMPLOYMENT HISTORY

St. Catherine's Hospital, Atlanta, Georgia

Level II RN

January 2004 to Present

Level II RN in 600-bed facility. Primary duties on pediatric floor; float to medical and surgical unit as needed to fill staffing shortages. Administer medications and assist staff physicians with treatment. Perform patient education and discharge planning responsibilities. Active member of volunteer training and quality control committees. Currently work part-time while completing M.S.N.

Page 1 of 2

EMPLOYMENT HISTORY, continued

Northeastern Community Hospital, Richmond, Virginia

Level II RN

May 2001 to January 2004

Level II RN in postoperative unit. Implemented various postoperative care plans. Supervised LPNs. Taught patient education classes. Performed discharge planning.

EDUCATION

M.S.N. Georgia State University, degree expected
June 2007

B.S.N. University of Virginia, March 2001

REFERENCES AVAILABLE

BILL K. WILLIAMSON

566 Courtney Lane
Uniondale, PA 18711
Cellular: 717-555-5958
Home: 717-555-8876

OBJECTIVE

Home health position using my prior oncology and cardiac experience.

WORK HISTORY

Uniondale General Hospital 1/04 to Present

Staff Nurse. Gained experience in cardiac, oncology, and pediatric units through working as a member of the float pool. Responsible for direct patient care, accurate and thorough electronic charting, creating care plans, and discharge planning.

Camenson Home Health 2/00 to 1/04

Case Manager. Coordinated and monitored patient care and progress. Scheduled home nursing care, ordered personal home equipment, arranged social services consults and support services as needed. Maintained and reviewed charts to ensure compliance with all federal and state health care regulations.

CREDENTIALS

• Pennsylvania Nursing License: RN384850

• Advanced Cardiac Life Support Certification

• Red Cross CPR Certification

• Member, American Society of Nurse Managers

EDUCATION

B.S.N. University of Washington—Seattle, 1/00

REFERENCES

Available on request

Karen Greenberg

486 Kramer Road, Uniondale, PA 18711
Home: (717) 555-8102   Cell: (717) 555-9988   E-mail: kgreen@xxx.com

Experienced RN with demonstrated skill in quality control, utilization review, cost containment, program coordination, and collaboration with both medical staff and hospital administration.

PROFESSIONAL EXPERIENCE

Hewlett Rehabilitation Center, Uniondale, PA
Educational Director, 2003 - Present
Responsible for all aspects of staff education for 320-bed hospital. Conduct utilization reviews. Develop guidelines for peer review and train supervisors in review strategies. Develop and implement training for new staff and in-service programs for existing staff. Create orientation manuals and supplementary educational materials. Monitor staff certification and licensure status, and schedule in-house certification programs in basic skills areas such as CPR.

Futura Home Health Inc., Cleveland, OH
Intake Supervisor, 2001 - 2003
Reviewed patient applications to determine needs and insurance eligibility. Took patient histories, reviewed medical records, and collaborated with hospital and nursing home discharge planners. Scheduled equipment deliveries and nursing, physical therapy, and social work visits. Created and updated individualized care plans. Conducted patient review meetings with staff. Hired, trained, and evaluated RNs, LPNs, and therapists for program.

Taft General Hospital, Cleveland, OH
Staff/Charge Nurse, 1999 - 2001
Staff RN and charge nurse for several departments, including medical/surgical, intensive care, and coronary care. Managed up to 35 patients and staff of up to five nurses and LPNs.

CERTIFICATIONS AND AFFILIATIONS

Member, National Council of Health Care Professionals, 2001
Delegate to national convention, 2003 - 2005

Member, Pennsylvania Nurses Association since 1999
Director, Membership Committee since 2002

Registered Nurse, Pennsylvania and Ohio since 1999

EDUCATION

B.S.N. Kent State University 1999

REFERENCES

Personal and professional references available.

KIRK FRANK

4316 Lincoln Street, Dallas, Texas 75243   (214) 555-9406   kfrank@xxx.com

Goal:
Finding the opportunity to combine my counseling skills and nursing education in a position as a crisis worker/RN in a hospital or clinical setting.

Skills:
- Volunteer recruitment and training
- Thorough knowledge of crisis intervention techniques
- Grief counseling experience
- Public relations and public speaking experience
- Fund-raising and grant-writing abilities
- Brochure and educational design skills

Employers:
Administrative Director, Kerrington Hospice
January 2006 to Present
Direct all activities for local hospice serving over 2,000 clients per year. Responsible for establishing annual budget, recruiting and training staff, organizing community relations activities, fund-raising, scheduling, counseling, and serving as liaison to local hospitals.

Director of Public Relations, Dallas General Hospital
May 2001 to January 2006
Responsible for producing hospital newsletter, representing hospital at community events, organizing community health programs, issuing press releases, and reporting to the press.

Education:
RN in progress, degree expected June 2008
Dallas General Hospital School of Nursing

B.A. in Communications, January 2001
Southern Methodist University

Computer Skills:
Microsoft Office
PageMaker
QuarkXpress
Photoshop

Affiliations:
National Society of Mental Health Practitioners
Student Nurses of America
Sigma Theta Tau, National Honor Society of Nursing Students

References:
On request

James K. Melton

784 Crest Avenue • San Antonio, TX 78284
Jamesmelton@xxx.com • (723) 555-1889

Goal
Management of daily operations and long-range planning for midsize medical clinic or nonprofit health care corporation.

Abilities
- Financial Planning
- Cost Containment
- Marketing
- Systems Analysis
- Grant Writing
- Setting Budgets

Work Experience
General Manager, 2005 - Present
Ridgeway Medical Clinic (San Antonio, TX)

Director, 2002 - 2005
Garner Medical Center (Dallas, TX)

Assistant Administrator, 2000 - 2002
Dallas Community Mental Health Program (Dallas, TX)

Education
M.B.A., University of Texas, 2000
RN, Larrabee School of Nursing, 1999

- Member, Texas Nurses Association
- Member, National Academy of Health Management
- Red Cross CPR Certification
- Texas Nursing License #214-476182

Technical Expertise
Proficient in Microsoft Office 2007, including Access, PowerPoint, Excel, and Word.

Familiar with PageMaker, Adobe Photoshop, and QuarkXpress. Also familiar with a variety of database management systems and other office management software.

References Available

Theodore (Ted) Le Mans, RN, M.S.N., CCNS

59 North Macon Street
Harlingen, TX 78550
Cellular Phone (210) 555-5968
E-mail tlm03@xxx.com

Overview

Nurse manager with ICU, CCU, and home health experience.
Coordinate scheduling and management of 15 employees for 20-bed
ICU. Ensure department's compliance with JCAHO standards and all
state and federal regulations. Monitor patients' treatment and status to
ensure quality pre- and postoperative care. Maintain quality control
standards through intensive orientation and ongoing program/service
development. Participated in committee for the successful application
for Magnet status.

Employers

6/02 - Present   Harlingen General Hospital—Harlingen, TX
Nurse Manager   Intensive Care Unit

5/99 - 6/02   Simpson Medical Center—Fort Worth, TX
Staff RN   Coronary Care Unit

6/97 - 5/99   Austin Home Health—Harlingen, TX
Case Manager

Credentials

Member, Nurse Manager's Association
Critical Care Nurse Specialist
M.S.N. Baylor University, 2001
B.S.N. Baylor University, 1997
Texas Nursing License 6817720-3

References Available

❖ STEPHANIE VERDE ❖

2002 WEST GRAYDON • CHICAGO, IL 60622
PHONE: (312) 555-8722 • E-MAIL: SVERDE@XXX.COM

❖ OBJECTIVE: Challenging career in the nursing field at a large metropolitan hospital or university medical center.

❖ EXPERIENCE:

July 2004–Present
Northwestern Memorial Hospital (NMH), Chicago, IL
Staff Nurse, Oncology/Hematology/Stem Cell Transplant
- Provide total patient care, medication, and chemotherapy administration, stem cell reinfusions, and patient and family support and education.
- Nursing care includes respiratory support, care of central venous access devices, blood draws and cultures, dressing changes, and interventions for graft-versus-host disease.
- Leadership activities in the form of committee participation and membership (see below).

August 2003–June 2004
Methodist Medial Center of Illinois, Peoria, IL
Nurse Technician, Oncology/Stem Cell Transplant Unit
- Provided total patient care with the exception of medication administration.
- Oversaw a full patient load under guidance of nurse preceptor.

December 2002–January 2003
Bradley University, Peoria, IL
Student Aide
- Planned and executed 13 freshman orientation sessions.
- Worked with a diverse team of 11 individuals to help students and families make a smooth transition to college.
- Conducted one-on-one interviews with freshmen, organized class schedules, and implemented student development workshops.
- Instructed EHS 120 "The University Experience" course with a member of the faculty.

❖ EDUCATION: Bradley University, Peoria, IL
                        Bachelor of Science in Nursing, 2004
                        Minors: Psychology, Health

❖ ACTIVITIES/LEADERSHIP:
- Member, NMH Medical Ethics Committee
- Member, NMH Blood Drive Committee
- Presenter, NMH Oncology Patient Education
- Panel Member, NMH Schwartz Center Ethics Rounds
- Medical Volunteer, Maison de Naissance, Torbeck, Haiti

❖ REFERENCES: Available on request

AUDREY WOODARD

946 Gates Street
McLean, VA 22102
(703) 555-6238
E-mail: nurseaudrey@xxx.com

OVERVIEW

B.S.N. with seven years of hospital nursing experience, seeking full-time staff RN position in medical/surgical unit. Seeking opportunity to grow into supervisory role. Willing to rotate shifts.

EXPERIENCE

New England General Hospital
Staff RN, Medical-Surgical Unit
1/03 to Present

Medical/surgical staff RN in 500-bed hospital. Rotate to other floors as needed. Active member of prevention of pressure ulcer and shared governance committees. Perform charge nurse duties as necessary, including scheduling, staff assignments, and addressing patients' and families' concerns.

Greenville County Hospital
Staff RN, Medical-Surgical/Orthopedic Unit
5/00 to 1/03

Provided primary care for postoperative patients. Supervised nursing students on clinical rotation. Spearheaded "Delirium Journal Club," educational group of nursing studying the literature on postoperative delirium.

CREDENTIALS

M.S.N., University of Vermont, expected date of graduation: 2008
B.S.N., University of Vermont, 2000
Member, American Nurses Association

REFERENCES

Available on request.

PATRICIA JOSEPH

913 Lincoln Street • Okeechobee, Florida 34972
(941) 555-3285 • E-mail: Patty345@xxx.com

Background

RN/EMT with extensive background in trauma services and fluent in Spanish. Seeking full-time ER nursing position.

Experience

6/2004 to Present
Wesley Memorial Hospital
ER nurse responsible for all phases of primary nursing care for level I trauma center receiving 30,000 visits annually. Triage patients and initiate treatment. Carry out physician's testing requests. Serve as committee member for quality assurance and volunteer training programs. Assisted with conversion from paper documentation to computerized charting using Powerchart documentation program.

5/2002 to 6/2004
Clark County Community Rescue Service
Emergency medical technician and team leader for mobile trauma unit. Stabilized patients in the field and transported to ER. Trained dispatchers. Regularly used Spanish-speaking skills, as area covered served primarily Latino population.

Education

Florida Nursing License 012-936474
RN Wesley Hospital School of Nursing—2004
A.S. Emergency Medical Technology, Punta Gorda Community College—2002

Certifications

Mobile Intensive Care Nurse (MICN)
Trauma Nurse Specialist (TNS)
Certified Emergency Nurse (CEN)
Certified Emergency Medical Technician (CEMT)
Certified CPR Instructor

Computer Skills

Extensive knowledge of Powerchart documentation program
Proficiency with Microsoft Office 2007

Affiliations

Emergency Nurses Association
Alliance of Trauma Care Providers

References Available

Lucy Wang

2411 Keystone Road

Madison, WI 53716

lucywang@xxx.com

Cellular: (608) 555-3445

Objective

RN position as a labor and delivery or postpartum care nurse.

Skills

- Assess and triage patients, both uncomplicated and high-risk deliveries
- Educate patients on pain management techniques during labor, postpartum care, and newborn care
- Assist physicians with deliveries
- Skilled lactation consultant
- Perform primary nursing duties in newborn nursery
- Create comprehensive discharge plans

Credentials

B.S.N. University of Wisconsin, 2001
Wisconsin Nursing License #86410
Labor and Delivery Nurse Specialist, 2004
Member, Association of Women's Health, Obstetric, and Neonatal Nursing

Employers

Madison Hospital
Madison, WI
Staff Nurse, Labor and Delivery
June 2003 - Present

Women's Health Cooperative
Madison, WI
Staff Nurse
July 2001 - June 2003

References

Personal and professional references on request.

Lisa P. Rogers

462 Reckert Road
East Hampton, NY 11937
lrogers22@xxx.com
(516) 555-7382

Goal

RN position on a pediatric general medical floor that allows me to combine my experiences working with children and addressing general medical patient needs.

Experience

Fairview Medical Clinic
Staff RN
6/05 to Present

Provide varied health care services at community clinic serving 20,000+ patients annually. Services include blood pressure screening, pregnancy and AIDS testing, routine prenatal services, TB screening, and psychiatric services and referrals. Use fluency in Polish language to communicate effectively with non-native English speaking clientele. Introduced Leininger's Culture Care Nursing Theory, which is now the clinic's guiding model of care.

School District 32
School Nurse
8/02 to 6/05

District nurse on call for three elementary schools. Maintained student health records on district mainframe. Dispensed medications, provided counseling, handled acute care situations with ease and authority. Organized district-wide wellness and parent education programs. Spearheaded successful "ABCs of Healthy Eating" campaign to remove junk foods from vending machines and cafeterias.

Credentials

B.S.N., East Hampton School of Nursing, 2002
-Graduated with Honors
A.S., Biology, New England Community College, 2000
Member, American Nurses Association

• References Available

Kimberly Rapley

1620 Coleman Road
Butte, MT 40112
(203) 555-2256
k_rapley@xxx.com

GOAL

Nursing Management Position

EXPERIENCE

First Street Women's Clinic
Clinical Coordinator, 1/01 to Present

Supervise nursing staff for women's clinic providing obstetric services and referrals for more than 500 patients per year. Hire, train, supervise, and evaluate nursing staff. Establish procedural standards. Reviewed charting and care plans to ensure compliance with all Medicare, Social Security, and Public Aid requirements.

St. Michael's Care Home
Staff Nurse, 1/98 to 1/01

Provided high-quality nursing care for residents of a 500-bed long-term care facility. Reviewed patients'

EXPERIENCE (continued)

medical status to make nursing diagnoses and develop and update individualized care plans. Established quality control program using patient satisfaction ratings as quality indicators.

CREDENTIALS

B.S.N. Pine Brook College, 1998
Certifications: CPR, ACLS, TNS, PALS
Montana License # 478-384759
Member, Montana Nurses Association
Member, American Nurses Association

REFERENCES

Available on request.

DENISE T. ROBINSON

3885 N. Hermitage Avenue, #1, Chicago, IL 60657
(773) 555-0655 • dtrobinson@xxx.com

OVERVIEW OF SKILLS

Exceptional communication, organizational, and time-management skills. Proven ability to handle multiple tasks. Collaborate effectively with others to accomplish a common goal. Display proficiency in nursing tasks, including assessment, planning, intervention, and evaluation. Earn excellent marks and high praise in clinical courses.

PROFESSIONAL EXPERIENCE

January 2006-present, *Graduate Nursing Student*

Successfully completed the following clinical courses:

- Obstetric nursing at St. Joseph Hospital
- Pediatric nursing at Children's Memorial Hospital
- Advanced physical assessment at Northwestern Memorial Hospital
- Medical-surgical nursing at Northwestern Memorial Hospital
- Psychiatric community nursing at C4 (outpatient program for individuals with schizophrenia)
- Fundamentals of nursing at Weiss Hospital

Demonstrate the following skills in patient care:

- Activities of daily living
- Ambulation and rotation
- Medication administration
- Specimen collection
- Assessment
- Plan of care
- Documentation
- Education and teaching

June 2006-present, *Nursing Assistant, Rush University Medical Center, Med/Surg Unit*

Provide patient care and hone organizational and time-management skills on a 37-bed unit serving renal (peritoneal dialysis and hemodialysis), cardiac monitoring/telemetry, respiratory, diagnostic, gastrointestinal, hematological, endocrine, and general neurological patients.

Page 1 of 2

PROFESSIONAL EXPERIENCE (continued)

January 2004-present, *Freelance Writer*

Revise and update career books. Write essays on a variety of topics spanning the humanities to science for K-8th grade educators.

December 2000-January 2004, *Editorial Assistant—Associate Editor, Sunshine Books*

Began publishing career as editorial assistant and earned greater responsibility and promotions. Acquired and managed quality projects from concept to publication in a variety of categories, including careers, self-help, parenting, popular culture, popular reference, health, and gift books.

EDUCATION

2004-present, *DePaul University—Chicago, Illinois*

Master's Entry to Nursing Practice program. Will graduate December 2008.

- 3.8 GPA
- Sigma Theta Tau, International Honor Society of Nursing, 2007
- Grace Peterson Scholarship, 2007
- Phi Theta Kappa, International Honor Society of the Two-Year College, 2002

1996-2000, *University of Michigan—Ann Arbor, Michigan*

Received a Bachelor of Arts, English

- Michigan Competitive Scholarship, 1996-2000
- Presidential Academic Achievement Award, 1996

VOLUNTEER ACTIVITIES

- St. Vincent DePaul Childcare Program, Spring 2007
- DePaul Foot Clinic, Spring 2007
- Advocate Illinois Masonic Hospital, December 2006, flu shot administration
- Northwestern Memorial Hospital, December 2000-April 2003, Jolly Trolley

REFERENCES

Available on request.

Elizabeth Carr

4820 South Engwall Road
Forsyth, GA 31209
(912) 555-4225

⊛⊛

Experience

Educational Consultant, October 2006 to Present
• Develop curriculum on contract basis. Recent clients include Forsyth Public Health
  Department and University of Georgia B.S.N. Program.

Assistant Professor of Nursing, September 2001 to October 2006
• Responsible for trauma nursing curriculum for University of Georgia's accredited
  B.S.N. program, with a course load of four sections per semester.
• Received superior student and staff evaluations.

Director of Nursing, August 1998 to September 2001
• Supervised nursing staff at St. Catherine's, a 500-bed facility.
• Carried out management and quality control responsibilities.

Staff Nurse, June 1995 to August 1998
• Provided direct patient care on a medical/surgical unit at New York University
  Downtown Hospital.

Education

M.S.N.   Syracuse University, New York 1995
B.A. (English)   University of Michigan, Ann Arbor 1990

Certifications

Georgia Public Health Certificate
Georgia Nursing License 628-543164
American Heart Association Certification for Basic and Advanced Life Support
Member, Emergency Nurses Association
ENA Trauma Nursing Core Provider
Patient Database Maintenance Certification

References

Personal and professional references provided on request.

JULIA SILVERMAN

453 Pratt Lane
Atlanta, Georgia 30301
(404) 555-3130
Pager: (404) 555-5674
juliesil@xxx.com

Objective:

Psychiatric nursing position, with eventual supervisory potential, in a hospital or clinic setting.

Work History:

2002 - Present   Level II RN
Atlanta General Hospital Psychiatric Services

- Provide all routine patient care.
- Dispense medication.
- Attend staff meetings.
- Assist with patient assessments.
- Assist with group therapy.
- Develop general care and discharge plans.

1999 - 2002   Staff Nurse
Covington House   Substance Abuse Program

- Assisted patients with emotional and physical problems related to substance abuse.
- Designed and implemented individualized rehabilitation programs.
- Served as admissions liaison to local hospitals.

1997 - 1999   Counselor
Mills Mental Health Center   Adolescent Mental Health

- Provided group and individual counseling to adolescents in crisis.
- Designed and presented in-service programs for high school counselors.

Education:

University of Georgia, B.S.N., 1997
Major: Nursing
Minor: Psychology
Licensed to practice nursing in the state of Georgia (#862-123026)

Affiliations:

Georgia Nurses Association • Southern Nurses Council

References:

On request.

ELENA PEREZ

2744 Covington Road
San Antonio, TX 78284
(210) 555-3964
E-mail: elenap@xxx.com

Nursing Skills

Primary care experience in neonatal ICU, newborn nursery, pediatric oncology unit, and pediatric medical/surgical unit.

Employers

St. Theresa's Hospital
Staff Nurse
Neonatal ICU
9/02 to Present
• Provide direct patient care for 6-bed unit, including critical care and life support measures
• Support respiratory function of premature infants
• Monitor cardiac complications

San Antonio Children's Hospital
Pediatric Staff Nurse
8/00 to 9/02
• Provided direct patient care for 20-bed unit

Lake Augusta Children's Camp
Summer Camp RN
5/98 to 8/00
• Provided first aid care to 500 adolescent campers
• Administered insulin and conducted blood glucose testing
• Taught children basic first aid and CPR

Credentials

B.S.N., Villanova University, 1998
Texas Nursing License #682-738914
PALS Certified
Member, Society of Pediatric Nurses

Personal and professional references on request.

STEVE WILSON

1062 West Lemont Road • St. Louis, MO 63146 • 314-555-2269

OVERVIEW
Nurse advocate and labor relations specialist. Act as a collective bargaining representative and health care lobbyist. Personally and professionally committed to furthering the best interests of registered nurses and licensed practical nurses to create a safe and productive health care environment.

EXPERIENCE
2004 - Present
Director, Missouri Nurses Association
Primary focus is drafting and lobbying for legislation to protect collective bargaining rights of nurses and LPNs.

2000 - 2004
Labor Relations Specialist, Midwest Nurses Alliance
Represented alliance members in grievance procedures and contract negotiations. Investigated grievances. Educated chairpersons to assist them in representing their bargaining units.

1995 - 2000
Educational Coordinator, Breslin Memorial Hospital
Responsible for staff orientation and certification programs, in-service workshops, nursing preceptor programs, and community health initiatives.

1990 - 1995
Staff Nurse, Breslin Memorial Hospital
Provided direct patient care on intensive care, medical/surgical, and oncology units. Conducted staff in-services covering a range of topics. Created educational seminars for families of patients facing a variety of issues and addressing numerous concerns.

PUBLICATIONS
• "Job Security in the Age of Downsizing," *The Nurse Advocate*, November 2006.
• "Collective Bargaining: The Newest Strategies," *Journal of Holistic Health*, July 2004.
• "The Politics of Public Policy," *American Nurse*, February 2001.

EDUCATION
M.S.N.	University of Texas Health Science Center	1995
B.S.N.	St. Catherine's College	1990

CERTIFICATIONS
National Labor Relations Board
ANCC Advanced Nursing Administration

REFERENCES
Available upon request.

JOSEPHINA VALENZUELA

B.S.N., M.S.N., CEN
9659 Dreyer Street
Santa Fe, NM 80204
E-mail: jvalenzuela@xxx.com
Pager: (303) 555-4507

Work History

4/01 to Present
Clinical Nurse Specialist/Nurse Manger
Kaiser Medical Center, Santa Fe, NM

Responsible for 24-hour management of emergency department services. Accountable for 25-bed ED with annual census of 40,000+ patients. Ensure best-practice standards of care. Coordinate activities and fiscal management of 50 employees. Ensure departmental compliance with hospital and JCAHO standards and regulations. Report directly to the assistant administrator.

3/99 to 4/01
Staff Educator
Jameson General Hospital, Santa Fe, NM

Worked in 40-bed ED/trauma center receiving 60,000 visits per year. Performed patient education, administered program/service development on hospital computer programs, and initiated quality improvement programs.

2/97 to 3/99
Trauma Nurse
Wexler Memorial Hospital, Santa Fe, NM

Triage and charge nurse for level I trauma center. Maintained a cool head and calm demeanor during crisis situations.

Education

M.S.N., University of New Mexico, 1999
B.S.N., University of New Mexico, 1997
TNS, CEN, ACLS certified
Member, Emergency Nurses Association

References

Personal and professional references available.

MARIE BURKE

5082 Merrick Street • Union, KY 41091 • Cellular: (606) 555-6315

Background

- B.S.N., working toward Master's degree
- Experience meeting the unique needs of pediatric and adolescent patients
- Diverse medical/surgical knowledge base
- Mental health counselor for psychiatric hospital

Employers

UNION HOSPITAL FOR CHILDREN
Staff RN
2004-Present

- Perform primary nursing duties for 30-bed pediatric unit. Rotate to med/surg unit as needed.

BRENTWOOD PSYCHIATRIC INSTITUTE
Mental Health Nurse
2002-2004

- General nursing, patient assessment, and counseling duties for psychiatric hospital specializing in pediatric and adolescent psych cases.

Education

- Kentucky Nursing License #484-123026
- M.S.N. in progress, Union College, degree expected 2008
- B.S.N., St. Catherine's College, 2002

Computer Skills

- Familiar with current computer programs used in regional medical facilities for documenting patient insurance information, recording stats, and logging medical history. Extensive work with patient database maintenance at Union Hospital. Also proficient in Microsoft Office 2007, including Word, Excel, Access, and PowerPoint.

REFERENCES AVAILABLE

✤ MARILYN SMITH

418 Whitesburg Street
Wauconda, IL 60084
847-555-9822
marilyn_smith@xxx.com

✤ OBJECTIVE

To obtain a nursing assistant position that will allow me to provide high-quality direct patient care in an orthopedic setting.

✤ EMPLOYMENT

2004 - Present
Nursing Assistant
Pinkerton Nursing Center, Gary, IN

Report to RNs regarding patients' status and current needs. Assist patients' activities of daily living, including self-care, eating, bathing, and grooming needs. Monitor and record fluid intake and output, vital signs, and general changes in mood or appearance. Ambulate patients and perform range of motion exercises. Promote patients' mental and physical health while assisting nursing staff.

2002 - 2004
Office Assistant
Kusler Medical Group, Merrillville, IN

Maintained database of patient files, answered phones, scheduled appointments, typed correspondence. Provided general clerical support for busy pediatric practice.

✤ EDUCATION

Nursing Assistant Certification
Columbia Vocational Institute, 2004

✤ COMPUTERS

Familiar with numerous word processing, presentation, and database programs, including Microsoft Office 2007 and Lotus Notes.

✤ REFERENCES

Available on request

SUSAN E. WILDER

962 Redmond Road • Melbourne, FL 32902 • 407-555-0179 • swilder@xxx.com

BACKGROUND

Nurse educator seeking tenure track assistant or associate professor position at nationally recognized nursing research university.

EXPERIENCE

Florida State University–Center for Nursing Practice
Assistant Professor of Nursing, 2002–Present
Responsible for maternal-child courses for RN-M.S.N. program. Clinical and lecture component. Consistently receive excellent student reviews. Mentor student research projects.

Melbourne Memorial Hospital
Education Specialist, 1998–2002
Implemented nursing orientation and preceptor programs. Developed and oversaw community health education programs. Presented in-services throughout the year. Oversaw annual competency reviews.

St. Francis Care Center
Director of Nursing, 1994–1998
Managed nursing staff for 50-bed substance abuse recovery program. Managed budget and balanced fiscal responsibilities with providing high-quality care.

RESEARCH

• Currently completing ongoing prevention and behavioral research at Florida State University regarding HIV-positive newborns.
• Recently awarded ANA grant to pursue research on clinical issues and trends in early intervention for developmentally delayed infants.
• M.S.N. research thesis: "Contraceptive Self-Efficacy and Teenage Mothers."

PUBLICATIONS

"Beating the Odds: Prenatal Care and Teenage Mothers," *American Nurse*, October 2005.
"Discharge Planning for the Addicted Newborn: Assuring Quality Care in the Home," *Social Services Weekly*, June 2003.

EDUCATION

M.S.N.	University of Missouri	1993
B.S.N.	Marycrest College	1989

CERTIFICATIONS

PALS	ACLS
CPR	TNS

References available on request.

Lisa K. Evans

1596 Piedmont Road

Durham, NH 03824

(603) 555-4206

levans@xxx.com

GOAL:

A staff nurse position at a clinic or hospital serving the geriatric patient population.

OVERVIEW:

• Talented RN with experience on orthopedic surgery ward
• Compassionate pre- and postoperative care
• Proven ability to develop successful discharge plans, including strategies for coping with altered mobility
• Nursing preceptor for new hires and student nurses

CREDENTIALS:

New Hampshire Nursing License #108-57410

RN, Durham School of Nursing, 2004

• Graduated with Honors
• 4.0/4.0 GPA

Member, American Nurses Association

Member, Sigma Theta Tau, International Honor Society for Nurses

WORK RECORD:

11/2004 to Present

Staff RN

Durham Community Hospital

Orthopedic Step-Down Unit

VOLUNTEER EXPERIENCE:

Planned Parenthood, 2000 to Present

Meals on Wheels, 2002 to 2005

Adopt a Grandparent, annual over Christmastime

References Available

Alexandra J. Kernig

483 West Fairfield Road
Santa Clara, CA 95051
Home: 408-555-1382
Pager: 408-555-5270
E-mail: akernig@xxx.com

GOAL: Nursing position with focus on serving post-trauma patient population. Interested in relocating to New York City or immediate vicinity. Able to work flexible hours.

EXPERIENCE: 4/2003 to Present
Santa Clara Rehabilitation Institute
Staff Nurse

Duties: General nursing responsibilities as member of multidisciplinary therapeutic team. Participate in development of treatment and discharge plans. Assess, monitor, and chart patient status. Assist physicians in performing diagnostic tests and providing treatment. Provide counseling, support, and education to patients and families.

9/2001 to 3/2003
Santa Clara YMCA
CPR Instructor

Duties: Trained community members in CPR techniques.

EDUCATION: B.S.N., St. Mary's College, March 2003
CPR and ACLS certification

LICENSE: California Nursing License #897-485757

AFFILIATIONS: California Nurses Association
American Nurses Association

REFERENCES AVAILABLE

SARA SAUNDERS

6204 Nessett Circle

Denver, CO 80262

(303) 555-7338 Home

(303) 555-1993 Office

E-mail: saunders@xxx.com

OVERVIEW

Experienced occupational health nurse with prior CCU experience. B.S.N. and critical care certifications along with eight years of nursing experience.

EXPERIENCE

Merrill Corporation
Occupational Health Nurse
2/05 to Present

Managed health care programs for corporation with more than 500 employees. Duties included pre-employment exams, documentation of workers' compensation cases, establishment of corporate safety standards, and creation and implementation of employee wellness programs.

Denver General Hospital
Staff Nurse, Critical Care Unit
2/00 to 2/05

Responsible for general nursing duties for critically ill surgical, coronary, and post-trauma patients.

EDUCATION

B.S.N., University of Colorado School of Nursing, 2000
ACLS Certified
TNS Certified

REFERENCES ON REQUEST

Paul Johnson, M.S.N.

296 Birkland Court • Conifer, CO 11535
(843) 555-7163 • pjohns11@xxx.com

Experience

9/06 to Present   **Project Manager**
Comprehensive Immunization Initiative
Colorado Nursing Foundation

Working to develop educational programs for health care professionals, design
public health programs, and establish goals for improved immunization service
and delivery to all children by age 24 months.

2/02 to 9/06   **Educational Specialist**
Helen White Nursing Scholar Program
National Nursing Academy

Assisted endowment director in reviewing scholarly abstracts to select
recipients of grants in public health nursing.

1/99 to 2/02   **Board Member**
Colorado Board of Nursing

Appointed to serve state nursing board consulting on professional issues,
including nursing licensure, disciplinary measures, school accreditation, and
establishment of nursing practices and procedures.

Education

M.S.N.   University of Denver   1999
B.S., Business   University of Denver   1997

REFERENCES AVAILABLE

INDIRA PAX

988 Gavin Road
Newport News, VA 23606
Home (904) 555-8214
Cellular (904) 555-9602

Goal:

Management position in home health industry that will use supervisory and marketing skills.

Experience:

9/04 to Present, Director of Recruitment, NurseTemps Inc.
• Direct marketing/recruitment program.
• Design direct mail campaigns.
• Produce promotional literature.
• Developed employee screening process currently in use.
• Monitor employee performance.
• Have increased staffing by 15 percent during past year.

8/00 to 9/04, Educational Director, St. Anne's Hospital
• Responsible for staff orientation, peer review, and community outreach programs.

7/96 to 8/00, Director of Nursing, Morgan County Hospital
• Supervised RN staff for 260-bed county hospital.
• Chaired shared governance and public health committees.

5/92 to 7/96, Level III RN, Morgan County Hospital
• Provided direct patient care on a 30-bed palliative care unit. Provided end-of-life care and symptom management. Conducted group grief counseling sessions to patients' family and friends.

Education:

M.S.N.	Wake Forest University	1996
B.S.N.	Western New England College	1992
A.A.	Newport Business College	1990

References:

On request.

Julia Templeton

2190 Emerson Street

Concord, MA 01742

(508) 555-5133

jtempleton@xxx.com

Areas of Nursing Expertise

- Oncology
- Hematology
- Cardiac Care
- Home Health

Skills

- ACLS and CEN certified with experience in cardiac care units
- Experienced oncology nurse, comfortable in both home health and hospital settings
- Proficient in administration of chemotherapy and IV therapy, including home setup of infusion pumps
- Skilled hematology nurse: draw blood; dispense whole blood, platelets, and cryoprecipitate; insert and maintain venous catheters

Employment

Home Health
Oakdale Home Health Care
2001 - Present
Home Health Oncology Nurse

Hospital
Liberty General Hospital
1999 - 2001
Staff Nurse

Hematology and Oncology
Health Temps
1997 - 1999
Agency Nurse

Education

University of Massachusetts B.S.N. 1997

References Available

Linda Abramo, RN

616 Winston Court

San Diego, CA 92123

Home: 619-555-1985

Cell: 619-555-7685

Objective: Full-time pediatric staff RN position in a hospital setting

Experience: Northwest Community Hospital
                   Pediatric Department
                   Staff Nurse, 6/05 to Present

• Provide primary nursing care for patients in 20-bed pediatric department.
• Support parents and families through therapeutic communication.
• Teach parents to change dressings, soothe children's fears of hospitals and
  healthcare workers, and properly administer medications.

                   Center for Child Protection
                   Catholic Children's Hospital
                   Staff Nurse, 7/01 to 6/05

• Staff RN for 50-bed pediatric unit specializing in child abuse recovery.
• Conducted therapeutic play services.
• Encouraged healthy expression of anger and fear.
• Prepared in-services to help staff deal with the trauma of seeing the results of
  child abuse.

Credentials: RN, Mercy Hospital School of Nursing, June 2001
                   California Nursing License #934-805413
                   PALS and CPR certified
                   Member, California Nurses Association

References: Available

TIM BRYANT

2130 Marquis Drive, St. Louis, MO 63146

Cellular: (816) 555-6277

E-mail: timbryant@xxx.com

CREDENTIALS

State of Missouri nursing license #687-358290

RN, Triton School of Nursing, 2000

Member, National Association of Orthopedic Nurses

CPR and ACLS Certified

WORK RECORD

Bennington Community Hospital

Orthopedic Staff Nurse

10/2005 to Present

Practice transcultural nursing and interdisciplinary collaboration to provide high-quality elder care for geriatric patients on an orthopedic surgical floor. Prepare patients for surgery and provide postoperative care. Assist patients with discharge planning and developing long-term strategies for dealing with the physical and emotional aspects of surgery. Implement study and treatment protocol for preventing falls associated with altered mobility.

Trenton Nursing Center

Staff Nurse

8/2000 to 10/2005

Provided skilled nursing care at 250-bed long-term care facility; experienced with geriatric Alzheimer's patients. Trained LPNs. Presented staff workshops on various topics, including "sundowning" syndrome in Alzheimer's patients and self-defense techniques for caregivers. Specialized in treating the psychosocial aspects of cognitive loss through evidence-based nursing practice. Conducted "Aging Sensitivity" exercises to explore staff's attitudes about aging and the elderly.

REFERENCES

Available on request.

KAREN A. FRASIER

5612 East Central Street
Ann Arbor, MI 48106
(313) 555-7614
kafrasier@xxx.com

GOAL

A nurse manager position in which I can use my extensive leadership skills and direct patient care experience for improving quality and performance on a cardiac or pediatric unit.

SKILLS

- Extensive background as Charge Nurse responsible for managing nursing staff to ensure prompt, high-quality nursing care.
- ER Triage Nurse with experience in assessing and prioritizing cases to facilitate smooth flow of patients and optimal use of nursing staff.
- Staff nurse positions in cardiac/telemetry and pediatric units.
- Active member of shared governance council.
- Arrange in-service presentations for nursing staff on varied topics, including self-defense for caregivers, HIV/AIDS updates, and child abuse detection.
- Knowledgeable in numerous computer programs for documenting patient history and stats; also proficient in Microsoft Word, Excel, and Access.

EMPLOYERS

Marist General Hospital
- ER Charge Nurse and Triage Nurse—July 2002 to Present

St. Mary's Hospital
  Staff Nurse:
- Cardiac/Telemetry Unit—May 1999 to July 2002
- Pediatric Unit—June 1997 to May 1999

CREDENTIALS

B.S.N., Michigan State University, awarded June 1997

TNS, ACLS, PALS, and CPR certified

Personal and professional references are available.

❖ Lisa Frankle

977 Calvert Road

Baltimore, MD 21202

lfrankle634@xxx.com

Home: (410) 555-1785

❖ Nursing Experience

9/96 to Present
St. Catherine's Hospital and Medical Center
Neonatal Nurse Practitioner

Provide primary care to newborns—well and ill—in neonatal ICU and newborn nursery. Accurately diagnose and treat this unique patient population. Provide care for the family unit as a whole. Emphasize education and teaching in practice and support parental decisions.

8/92 to 9/96
Garrett Children's Hospital
Pediatric Staff Nurse

Provided primary care for pediatric patients in 200-bed children's hospital. Acquired extensive oncology and medical/surgical experience while working in the float pool.

5/89 to 8/92
Morgan Medical Group
Pediatric Nurse

Provided primary care for private pediatric practice. Provided emotional support and teaching to families. Conducted family wellness seminars on nutrition and safety issues.

❖ Education

B.S.N., University of Baltimore   1989

❖ Affiliations

Society of Pediatric Nurses
Maryland Nurses Association

❖ References

On request

CECILIA RUIZ

1921 WILLOWBROOK ROAD

(314) 555-1170

COLUMBIA, MO 65212

CRUIZ@XXX.COM

Goal
A position in nursing management in an emergency room setting, which would allow me to use my critical thinking skills and significant trauma experience to lead others.

Highlights
- M.S.N., Nurse Practitioner from University of Virginia, 2000
- B.S.N., University of Virginia, 1995
- Licensed in Virginia (#118-142037) and Missouri (#868-347124)
- Five years of clinical experience
- CPR and ACLS certified
- Nursing instructor and educator

Employment

2006 - Present	Trauma Nursing Instructor Columbia School of Nursing Columbia, MO
2003 - Present	Trauma Services Coordinator Mosby Hospital Columbia, MO

Employment (continued)

2000 - 2003   Nurse Practitioner
St. John's Medical Center
Richmond, VA

1995 - 2000   Level III Trauma Nurse
Children's Hospital
Washington, DC

Achievements

- Manage 10 RNs, LPNs, and support staff at 200-bed regional medical center
- Served as delegate to Emergency Nurses Association Conference, 2000 and 2001
- Presented paper, "Pediatric Cardiovascular Emergencies," at ENA Scientific Assembly, 2003
- Received Award for Professionalism from Mosby Hospital Board of Directors, 2006

References

Provided on request

MACKENZIE JONES

439 Washington Street
Charleston, South Carolina 29425
Home: 803-555-4671
mackj@xxx.com

Background

Nursing experience in hospital ICU and medical/surgical units. B.S.N. plus critical care certifications.

Skills

- Primary patient care, including IV therapy, monitoring of vital signs, post-operative wound care, and pain management.
- Delegation to and supervision of nursing assistants; orientation of new staff; and monitoring of nursing students.
- Extensive voluntary participation in hospital's community-based health care programs, including blood drives, mobile immunization efforts, and public speaking engagements.
- Fluent in Spanish.

Employers

Charleston Medical Center
Staff Nurse
2/05 to Present

Education

B.S.N. South Carolina State College, 2005
- Graduated with honors
Certifications: TNS, CEN, ACLS

References available.

AMANDA HARDING

1910 Hardy Street • Honolulu, Hawaii 96814 • Home: 808-555-6668 • E-mail: aharding2@xxx.com

Goal

Nursing program management responsibilities in either a clinic or a hospital setting using my skills in mental and public health nursing.

Work History

Keahou Clinic, Honolulu, Hawaii
Substance Abuse Counselor, 2005 - Present
Provide one-on-one and group counseling to adolescent clients in private substance abuse treatment program. Recruit and train volunteers for crisis hotline. Develop and present educational programs at local high schools to encourage students to remain drug-free.

Edgewater Hospital, Sacramento, California
Managing Director, Outpatient Mental Health Clinic, 2001 - 2005
Staff RN, 1999 - 2001
Directed outpatient mental health program serving approximately 80 clients per year. Program provides outpatient counseling, monitors patients' drug and psychotherapy regimes, and assists with placement in supervised living situations. Duties included staffing, scheduling, and giving reports to attending psychiatrists. Promoted after serving two years as staff RN in program, taking histories and assisting with office management.

Clayton Associates, Sacramento, California
Staff RN, 1995 - 1999
Staff RN for physicians group in general practice. Assisted with direct patient treatment: charted status, took histories, provided treatment; assisted with patient scheduling as needed; provided home care instructions.

Arrowhead School, Monterey, California
School Nurse, 1990 - 1995
Provided on-site routine and acute care as needed and assisted with ongoing health programs. Maintained students' health care files; provided health bulletins for parents and guardians.

Education

Licensed in the states of California (427-583215) and Hawaii (661-326335)

RN   Monterey School of Nursing 1990

B.S. Kenyon College, Psychology 1988

References

Personal and professional references provided on request.

Trudy P. Miller

411 Greenville Road

Eau Claire, Wisconsin 54702

TPMiller@xxx.com

715-555-9712

GOAL:

Medical Services Coordinator

SKILLS:

- Financial management and fund-raising experience
- Knowledge of JCAHO accreditation standards, state and federal guidelines
- Creation of procedural standards, quality control programs
- Knowledge of Medicare, Social Security, and Public Aid regulations
- Familiar with various computer programs to maintain patient files and insurance database

EMPLOYERS:

Stevenson Rehabilitation Clinic
Discharge Planner
1/05 to Present

Northeast Community Hospital
Patient Liaison
1/00 to 1/05

CREDENTIALS:

M.S.N., University of Wisconsin, Whitewater, 2005
B.A., English, University of Michigan, 2001
Certifications: CPR, CEN, TNS, ACLS
Member, American Nurses Association

REFERENCES:

Available on request

SHANDELL BROWN

682 Paxton Street • Grand Rapids, MI 49505
Cellular: 312-555-9684 • sbrown@xxx.com

Background
Professional RN with hospital nursing and home health experience. Seeking challenging staff nurse position with potential to grow into supervisory duties.

Skills
- Experienced oncology nurse familiar with plasmapheresis, pain control and symptom management, and counseling for terminally ill patients and their families
- Case management experience acquired as home health and private-duty nurse working to coordinate with community resources and services to ensure comprehensive patient care plans
- IV therapist
- ICU nurse capable of assessing and responding to cardiac emergencies

Work History
2002 - Present	Spectrum Community Hospital ICU & Oncology Units	Level II RN
2000 - 2002	Jessup Personnel	Private-Duty Nurse

Education
RN, Kalamazoo School of Nursing, 2000
License: Michigan #283-394857

Certifications
CPR
Advanced Cardiac Life Support
Oncology Certified Nurse

Affiliations
Michigan Nurses Association
National Council for Home Health Professionals
Oncology Nurses Society

Computer Skills
Proficient in Microsoft Office 2007, including Word, Excel, Meeting Maker, and PowerPoint. Also knowledgeable in numerous database programs used in area hospitals for tracking patient stats and history.

References
On request

Ellen O'Shea

724 Olympia Drive
Des Moines, IA 50265
Home: (319) 555-1284
Cell: (319) 555-6744

Overview

Licensed Iowa RN with experience in private practice and community health. Excellent interpersonal, communication, and marketing skills. Strong rapport with patients. Holistic approach to health care.

Work Experience

Planned Parenthood, Des Moines, IA
Reproductive Counselor
2004 - Present
Provide reproductive counseling at walk-in clinic serving 500+ clients per year. Provide one-on-one patient education regarding birth control and pregnancy. Assist with general office management, including patient scheduling and maintenance of computer database and files. Participate in short- and long-term planning of program. Monitor changes in federal health care law and implement procedural changes as necessary.

LifeSource, Des Moines, IA
Blood Drive Coordinator
2001 - 2004
Contacted corporations to request off-site blood drives. Set up equipment and supervised blood drives at corporate sites. Took donor histories, supervised LPNs and RNs, provided discharge instructions to donors. Assisted with in-house donations as necessary, including patient intake, scheduling, and telemarketing efforts to increase donations.

Capital Medical Group, Iowa City, IA
Staff Nurse
1999 - 2001
General-duty nurse for pediatric practice. Provided standard well-baby care, such as immunizations and oral polio treatments, as directed by physicians. Took patient histories, assessed and charted conditions, completed necessary paperwork, and maintained patient files.

Education

University of Iowa
B.S.N., Public Health, 1999

References

Available on request

Margaret Sweeney, RN

220 Prospect Street

McLean, VA 22102

(703) 555-7815

msweeney@xxx.com

Work History

2003 - Present
Briar Street Clinic
Level II Staff Nurse. Provided routine outpatient care, community referral, and counseling at medical clinic averaging 20,000 visits annually.

2000 - 2003
McLean General Hospital
Level II Pediatric Staff Nurse. Acquired extensive experience with pediatric oncology cases. Adept at plasmapheresis, IV therapy, pain control, symptom management, and grief counseling.

1998 - 2000
Gannon Medical Center
Level II RN, Neonatal ICU. Provided clinical nursing assessment and appropriate interventions for critically ill infants.

Education

M.S.N.   University of Vermont   2000
B.S.N.   University of Vermont   1998

Certifications/License

Pediatric Advanced Life Support Certified
CPR Certified
RN License 862-503126

Affiliations

Virginia Nurses Association
Society of Pediatric Nurses

References available on request

JEFFREY FRANCIS

202 Bedford Lane
Roselle, Illinois 60172
(630) 555-8162 Home
(630) 555-3571 Cellular

Background: Professional health care manager who provides sound business leadership while creating an environment conducive to compassionate patient care.

Skills:

Business

- Sales
- Marketing
- Budgetary Control
- Purchasing

Supervisory

- Employee Recruitment
- Training
- Performance Evaluations
- Scheduling

Employers: 2000 - Present

Director, Harrison Home Health

Elmhurst, Illinois

Direct all aspects of agency. Develop and implement marketing plan. Ensure compliance with all state and federal regulations. Purchase all durable medical equipment. Develop and monitor annual budget.

1996 - 2000

Personnel Director, St. Catherine's Skilled Care Center

Mount Prospect, Illinois

Responsible for all aspects of human resources for staff of 20+ health care workers. Duties included hiring, training, supervising, scheduling, and evaluating employees.

Page 1 of 2

Employers: 1993 - 1996
(continued)   *Level III RN, Rosary Hospital*
Park Ridge, Illinois
Provided direct patient care in pediatrics and medical/surgical departments.

Education: B.S.N., University of Illinois, Chicago, 1993
Minor in Accounting

Affiliations: Illinois Nurses Association
Society of Health Care Managers

References: Available on request

SOPHIE BURGESS

245 Bishop Street
Boulder, Colorado 80303
303-555-1936
sburgess@xxx.com

OBJECTIVE

Seeking part-time employment in the dynamic field of home health care.

EXPERIENCE

Wesley Memorial Hospital
512 Cutler Street
Denver, Colorado 80209

2004 - Present
Charge Nurse for 10-bed Acute Coronary Care Unit with 50 percent patient turnover daily

- Extensive experience with ventilators, intra-aortic balloon pumps, Swan-Getz catheters, and cardiac rhythm identification.
- Proficient in IV insertion, infusion of vasoactive drugs, phlebotomy, and 12-lead EKGs.
- Cross-trained to assist in six different units: surgical intensive care, endocrine/GI, pulmonary/renal, general surgical, monitored cardiac rehabilitation, and outpatient pulmonary/cardiac rehabilitation.
- Successfully implement cost-containment procedures, resulting in a 90 percent reduction of lost revenue.
- Delegate responsibilities as needed in role of charge nurse.

2001 - 2004
Level II RN for Acute Dialysis Plasmapheresis Unit

- Conducted in-services on pain assessment, radiological assessment of line placement, and physicians' order entry system.
- Served as a delegate to the American Nephrology Nurses Association National Conference, 1992, in Washington, DC.

EXPERIENCE (continued)

1998 - 2001
Staff Nurse for 6-bed Intensive Care Unit

• Provided primary care to critically ill adult patients suffering from a wide range of diseases.

EDUCATION

Received Associate's Degree in Nursing Science from Truman City College in 1998. Earned 80 percent of educational expenses working part-time while maintaining full course loads. Currently pursuing B.S.N. through Colorado University.

CERTIFICATION

ACLS and CPR certified

OTHER

Currently work one shift a month in pulmonary cardiac rehabilitation.

References Are Available

Marguerite Kusaka

3984 Briar Street
Oakland, California 94609
Home: (414) 555-2837
Cell: (414) 555-0098
E-mail: mkusaka@xxx.com

EXPERIENCE

General Manager
St. Mary's Medical Center
Oakland, California
2002 - Present
Direct day-to-day operations and long-range planning for medical clinic with annual budget of $2.5 million. Areas of responsibility include financial planning, cost containment, and staffing.

Achievements
- Increased first-year profits by 10 percent
- Continue to maintain steady financial growth
- Implemented marketing plan that resulted in a 15 percent increase in patient referrals from private physicians

Assistant Director
Lakehurst Recovery Center
San Francisco, California
1999 - 2002
Supervised medical records, admissions, and billing departments for substance abuse center with staff of 60.

Achievements
- Streamlined billing procedures
- Reduced annual operating expenses by 5 percent

EXPERIENCE *(continued)*

Assistant Administrator
Northwest Mental Health Center
Berkeley, California
1997 - 1999
Assisted general manager of 60-bed psychiatric center. Participated in all aspects of health management: educational, therapeutic, and personnel. Involved in hiring and training of new staff members and volunteers. Assisted in direct patient care and emergency intervention as needed. Responsible for all billing.

Achievements
- Successfully recruited and trained group of 12 new volunteers
- Secured a $250,000 federal grant for research in obsessive-compulsive disorders
- Implemented HELP computer program for the entire center

EDUCATION

M.S. in Public Health Administration, 1993
University of Hawaii

B.S. in Psychology, 1990
University of California, Berkeley

AFFILIATIONS

California Public Health Council
American Management Association
National Academy of Office Administrators

REFERENCES

Available on request

JESSICA STILSON, RN

411 HIGHLAND COURT

BROOKINGS, SD 57007

HOME: (605) 555-3889

CELL: (605) 555-9866

EMPLOYMENT HISTORY

2005 - Present
Director, Corneal Transplant Program
South Dakota State University Eye Clinic

Manage corneal transplant program. Duties include tracing donors through nationwide computer database, supervising tissue typing, arranging the harvesting and transport of donor organs, counseling donor families, and obtaining formal consents. Direct clerical staff of two. Designed and implemented community outreach plan to increase awareness of need for donor organs.

2001 - 2005
Level III Trauma Nurse
St. Patrick's Hospital, Emergency Department

Provided full range of trauma nursing services in emergency department with annual census of 25,000 patients. Facilitated SDSU organ donations when possible, counseling families and securing initial consents. Developed in-service program to educate staff on obtaining organ donation consents.

Page 1 of 2

EMPLOYMENT HISTORY (continued)

1998 - 2001
Level II Staff Nurse
St. Patrick's Hospital, Neonatal Intensive Care

Provided direct patient care to critically ill newborns in six-bed neonatal intensive care unit. Assessed, monitored, and charted patient status. Implemented treatments and administered medications as directed. Provided patient education and emotional support for family members.

EDUCATION

B.S.N.   South Dakota State University   1998

CERTIFICATIONS

• TNS, Trauma Nurse Specialist Certification
• CEN, Certified Emergency Nurse
• ACLS, Advanced Cardiac Life Support
• South Dakota State Nursing License #345-687958

REFERENCES

Both personal and professional references are available upon request.

Maria Ramos, M.S.N.

986 Yates Street • Chicago, IL 60618 • Home: (312) 555-6978
Cell: (312) 555-3999 • E-mail: ramos_maria@xxx.com

Work History

1/02 to Present, Director of Education and Community Relations
Bradley Medical Center
- Develop and implement all staff training, in-service programming, recertification programs.
- Supervise publication of in-house newsletter, press releases, and patient education literature.
- Design and direct marketing/community relations campaigns and special events.
- Serve as media contact/hospital spokesperson.

10/98 to 1/02, Director
Ridgeway Rehabilitation Center
- Directed daily operation of 50-bed residential substance abuse treatment center.
- Managed nursing and support staff.
- Assisted board of directors with long- and short-range budgets and planning.
- Directed fund-raising and community relations efforts.

8/98 to 10/01, Assistant Professor
St. Andrews College, B.S.N. Program
- Taught public health nursing, pediatric nursing, and chemical dependency courses in a part-time position.
- Functioned as research assistant.
- Assumed responsibility for ongoing curriculum development.

6/94 to 8/98, Staff Nurse
Children's Hospital
- Served as pediatric staff RN for 250-bed hospital.
- Garnered a wide range of experience, including trauma, burn, and oncology cases.

Computer Proficiency

MS Word, Excel, Outlook   Quicken
Powerchart   Adobe Illustrator

Education

M.S.N.   University of Illinois   1998
B.S.N.   University of Delaware   1994

References available on request.

CLARENCE T. JACKSON

3316 Westview Road
Lake Forest, CA 92630
tjackson@xxx.com
(714) 555-6150

OVERVIEW

Experienced EMT capable of responding to wide variety of trauma cases at scene. Currently seeking RN licensure. Strong commitment to career in trauma services.

EDUCATION

B.S., Nursing
University of California
Degree expected 2008

A.S., Emergency Medical Technology
Lake Forest Community College
2002

- Board-Certified EMT
- CPR Instructor

EXPERIENCE

Lake Forest Community Rescue Team   2002 to Present
Team leader for urban mobile trauma unit. Interface with hospital ER staff by phone to provide trauma management en route from accident scenes. Stabilize patients for transport. Train dispatchers to answer calls and document critical information.

Warren County Fire and Rescue Service   2000 to 2002
CPR instructor for firefighters and EMTs. Provided CPR certification programs for community groups as requested.

REFERENCES AVAILABLE

TRICIA SANSONE

6576 Elizabeth Court

Falmouth, MA 02541

Home: (508) 555-8325

Office: (508) 555-9415

BACKGROUND

• Experienced hospital administrator

• Strong employee relations and arbitration skills

• Proven record of cost containment and quality control

• Successful facilities manager

WORK HISTORY

2000 - Present

Administrative Director

Falmouth General Hospital, Falmouth, MA

• Assist chief administrator in directing all activities of this 300-bed facility. Duties include personnel management, fiscal management, and public relations.

Achievements

• Initiated fund-raising effort that increased hospital endowment by $1.5 million.

• Designed new community outreach projects to enhance hospital's visibility and image in the community.

WORK HISTORY (continued)

1995 - 2000
Assistant Hospital Administrator
Perkins Memorial Hospital, Richmond, VA
• Responsible for fiscal management, human resources, and facilities management projects under supervision of chief administrator.

Achievements
• Instituted new data processing procedures that increased collections and facilitated third-party reimbursements.
• Directed construction of $25 million maternal/child care wing that increased admissions by 20 percent.
• Responsible for all aspects of project: funding, contract negotiations, project management.
• Project completed on time and within budget.

EDUCATION

M.B.A. Harvard University, 1994
B.S.N. University of Virginia, 1990

References Available

GEORGIA BETTS

1037 West Robin Road
Austin, TX 78768
(512) 555-8718
gbetts@xxx.com

EMPLOYMENT

2006 - Present   St. Joseph's Hospital
                    Emergency Department RN Level III
- Responsible for all aspects of direct patient care at this level I trauma center with annual census of 32,000 patients
- Preceptor for new employees
- Public safety liaison
- Active member of education, public safety, and certification committees; coordinated in-service presentations on topics such as domestic violence, elder abuse, AIDS education, and self-defense for caregivers

2002 - 2006   Hennessey Hospital Medical Center
                 Emergency Department RN
- Direct patient care
- Extensive community referral
- Liaison to community mental health center affiliated with the hospital

1999 - 2002   Hennessey Hospital Medical Center
                 Medical/Surgical RN
- Responsible for general pre- and postoperative care on 30-bed floor

CERTIFICATIONS/LICENSE

Advanced Cardiac Life Support (ACLS)
Certified Emergency Nurse (CEN)
Trauma Nurse Specialist (TNS)
Mobile Intensive Care Nurse (MICN)
Texas Nursing License #062-778019

EDUCATION

Hennessey Hospital School of Nursing, RN, 1999

AFFILIATIONS

Member, Emergency Nurses Association
Texas Nurses Association

References available on request

Madison Browne

418 Bradley Street • Bay City, MI 48706
517-555-5967 • madisonbrowne@xxx.com

OVERVIEW

Licensed RN and labor relations specialist with diverse experience in health education. Interested in challenging in-house position with nursing association or union.

WORK HISTORY

2005–Present
Labor Relations Specialist
Self-employed labor relations specialist. Participate in contract negotiations as the collective bargaining representative for RNs. Successfully negotiated four labor agreements during the past year, all including an increase in hourly wages.

2001–2005
President • Michigan Nurses Association
Directed professional nursing organization with 5,500 members and an annual budget of $250,000. Recruited members, supervised publication of monthly newsletter, directed daily operation of office, and coordinated continuing education efforts and special events.

1998–2001
Educational Director • Lutheran General Hospital
Managed all educational programs. Developed orientation materials and in-service programming. Monitored staff certification and provided recertification programs in-house and off-site. Supervised production of in-house newsletter and patient education literature.

1995–1998
Part-Time Lecturer • Saginaw College B.S.N. Program
Taught maternal and child care courses in accredited B.S.N. program. Responsible for two sections and up to 40 students per semester. Received excellent student and peer reviews.

QUALIFICATIONS

M.S.N.   Wayne State University   1998
B.S.N.   Central Michigan University   1993
Michigan Nursing License: 411-608542
National Labor Relations Board Certification
Member, American Nurses Association
Member and Past President, Michigan Nurses Association

REFERENCES

Available on request.

MARK D. BRADLEY

5895 GLENDALE ROAD

LAKE FOREST, CA 92630

(714) 555-4956

Work Experience

Nursing

- Level III staff RN for level II trauma/emergency department
- ICU/CCU experience on part-time, on-call basis
- Home health experience
- Quality assurance specialist

Teaching

- Instructor, Mobile Intensive Care Nurse course
- Curriculum consultant for Lake Forest Department of Public Health's paramedic training program

Supervision

- Charge nurse for level II trauma center
- Relief house supervisor for level II trauma center

Employers

Holy Cross Hospital	Level III Staff RN	1/05 to Present
Barrington Home Health	Agency RN	8/02 to 1/05
Alexis Medical Center	Charge RN	8/99 to 8/02

Education

B.S.N.   University of California, San Diego, 2004
A.S.   Lakeland College, 1999

Certifications

California Nursing License: RN495860

Basic and Advanced Life Support, American Heart Association

Certified Emergency Nurse

Trauma Nursing Core Provider

Emergency Nurses Association

Member, California State Nurses Association

References available on request.

BARBARA TURKINGTON

1950 South Union Street

Melbourne, FL 32901

bturk@xxx.com

407-555-8237

OBJECTIVE:

Triage Nursing Position in Trauma/ER Department

SKILLS:

- Document patient histories and status in various computer programs and databases
- Exercise sound judgment as triage nurse responsible for prioritizing cases and assigning staff
- Provide medical advice and poison control information by phone
- Initiate patient treatment and testing
- Schedule staff members and ensure adequate departmental staffing

EMPLOYERS:

Melbourne General Hospital, Triage Nurse—April 2002 to Present

Wharton Medical Center, Staff Nurse—May 1998 to April 2002

Lincoln Medical Center, Nursing Assistant—June 1993 to May 1998

EDUCATION:

RN, St. Andrew's School of Nursing, 1998

References available

✦ TAMARA FOSTER, Pediatric Nurse Practitioner

494 Brook Street
West Lafayette, Indiana 47907
317-555-8460
E-mail: tamara_foster@xxx.com

✦ Experience

Southwest Community Mental Health Service
Psychiatric Nurse Practitioner
2/04 to Present
Provide outpatient therapy at community mental health center. Responsible for 24-hour emergency service rotation; provide education and consultation to health care professionals and family caretakers.

Preston Adolescent Treatment Center
Level II Staff RN
6/01 to 2/04
Member of multidisciplinary treatment team serving adolescent women dealing with mental health issues, including substance abuse and eating disorders. Duties included patient observation and assessment, nursing diagnosis, care planning, counseling, and crisis intervention.

Hoffman House
Staff RN, 8/95 to 6/01
Staff RN for adult respite care center. Varied patient population included seniors with memory loss and limited mobility. Ensured safe, therapeutic environment for clients. Provided education and emotional support for primary caregivers.

✦ Education

M.S.N., NP—Purdue University, 2004
B.S.N.—Purdue University, 1995

✦ Affiliations

American Nurses Association
Midwest Alliance of Nurse Practitioners

✦ References Available

Betsy Lindquist

625 South Henderson Street
Falmouth, MA 02541
(508) 555-1068
Cell: (508) 555-7364
E-mail: lindquistb@xxx.com

Objective:

Occupational Health Nursing Position

Skills:

• Administer preemployment physical exams
• Test physical work ability
• Evaluate workers' compensation claims
• Assess workplace safety
• Develop and administer employee fitness and wellness programs
• Administer health care benefits programs
• Microsoft Office 2007
• Lotus Notes

Employers:

New England Nurses Association
Workplace Advocate   6/04 to Present

The Leland Corporation
Occupational Nurse   8/00 to 6/04

Credentials:

B.S.N., Medical University of South Carolina, College of Nursing, 2000
Member, American Nurses Association

References Available

SUSAN WRIGHT

1411 Harrod Lane
Boulder, CO 80304
Home: 303-555-4958
Pager: 303-555-6789
E-mail: suewright@xxx.com

GOAL

Entry-level RN position building on my experience as a nursing assistant.

EXPERIENCE

2006 to Present
Volunteer Nursing Assistant
Mercy Hospice

• Assist nursing staff in providing primary care to terminally ill patients.
• Monitor patients' status and vital signs and report to nursing supervisor.
• Provide grooming and bathing assistance and emotional support for patients.

2002 to 2006
Medical Records Clerk
Bishop Hospital

• Recorded patient histories and insurance information.
• Maintained computerized patient database.
• Gained extensive knowledge of medical terminology.

EDUCATION

Florence Nightingale School of Nursing, A.S., 2003
RN expected June 2007

CREDENTIALS

CPR certified
Member, American Student Nurses Association

References available on request.

Anne Quincy

488 Sterling Road

Richmond, KY 40475

Home: (606) 555-2067

Cell: (606) 555-7292

E-mail: annequincy@xxx.com

Background

B.S.N. with experience in both hospital and home health settings. Oncology and cardiac care background. Ten years of nursing experience.

Experience

Richmond Community Medical Center
Staff Nurse, Oncology Unit   6/04 to Present

Responsible for all direct patient care including setup of infusion pumps, IV therapy, chemotherapy, and pain management. Educate and counsel patients and families. Interact extensively with radiologists and respiratory therapists.

Page 1 of 2

Experience (continued)

St. Francis Hospital
Staff Nurse, Cardiac Care Unit   8/00 to 6/04

Responsible for direct care of cardiac patients. Proficient in IV therapy, use of ventilators, intra-aortic balloon pumps, Swan-Getz catheters, and 12-lead EKGs. Assisted in Cardiac Rehabilitation Unit as requested.

Regency Nursing Agency
Per Diem RN   8/97 to 8/00

Agency nurse responsible for long- and short-term private-duty assignments serving a wide array of patients.

Education

B.S.N.   Eastern Kentucky University   1997

References Available

CHRISTINE ANDERSON

1811 Foley Street #6028 • Washington, DC 20024

(202) 555-4113 • E-mail: canderson@xxx.com

Overview

RN with background as program coordinator and educational director desires position as educational director for local hospital or medical research foundation.

Employers

2004 - Present
Education Director
American Nurses Association
Washington, DC

2001 - 2004
Director of Development
Lexington Home Health Care
Lexington, KY

1998 - 2001
Staff RN
Richmond General Hospital
Richmond, VA

Skills

Public and media relations
Curriculum development
Nursing recruitment, orientation, and
management

Computer Knowledge
- Microsoft Office 2007 (Word, Excel, Outlook)
- Lotus Notes
- PageMaker
- QuarkXpress
- Familiarity with Internet search engines and
  online medical databases

Education

M.Ed.   Georgetown University   2001
B.S.N.   University of Virginia   1998

References available on request

◆ VANESSA SMITH

4182 Victoria Street
Dublin, CA 94568
Home: 510-555-7796
Cell: 510-555-2120
E-mail: vanessa_smith@xxx.com

◆ OBJECTIVE

Community mental health nursing position in hospital or clinic setting

◆ EXPERIENCE

1/04 to Present
Dublin General Hospital and Medical Center
Crisis Counselor, Outpatient Mental Health

Provide group and individual counseling services in outpatient clinic. Responsible for 24-hour emergency rotation, recruitment, and training of volunteers. On call for ER to assist with clinical assessment of psychiatric cases, referral, and/or facilitation of transfer to appropriate facility.

◆ EXPERIENCE (continued)

5/02 to 1/04
Mercy Hospice
Grief Counselor

Counseled terminally ill patients and families. Oriented new staff members. Participated in community outreach, public speaking engagements, and fund-raising. Served as an advocate for rights of the terminally ill.

◆ EDUCATION

California Nursing License #218-730614

M.S.W.	Rosary College	2002
RN	College of St. Catherine	1999

◆ REFERENCES AVAILABLE

Kevin Riley

622 Robinson Road

Des Plaines, IL 60016

(847) 555-6123 Home

(847) 555-8127 Work

kriley@xxx.com

Goal: Teaching position with university or educational foundation.

Expertise: Nursing experience in hospital and clinic settings. Member of multidisciplinary rehabilitation team for patients with spinal cord injuries. Nursing supervisor for hospital and outpatient substance abuse programs. Teaching and curriculum development experience at the university level. Implementing new technology and training staff on effective archiving. Clinical researcher conducting ongoing analysis of the effect of behavior modification techniques on substance abuse.

Credentials: M.S. in Nursing, University of Florida, 1994
B.S.N., Central Florida University, 1990
Member, American Nurses Association

Page 1 of 2

Employers: 2002 - Present
Assistant Professor
Elmhurst College B.S.N. Program
Teach psychosocial nursing, medical ethics, and research methods. Supervise nursing students in on-site clinical rotations. Conduct extensive research. Have input into department's ongoing curriculum development.

1998 - 2002
Nursing Supervisor
Rehabilitation Institute of Daytona
Supervised staff of 30 RNs at rehabilitation facility providing comprehensive care for patients recovering from spinal cord injuries. Developed care plans in conjunction with psychology, occupational therapy, and physical therapy professionals. Responsible for staff scheduling, evaluations, in-service presentations, patient education, and discharge planning.

1994 - 1998
Head Nurse
Lambert Treatment Center
Nursing supervisor for outpatient substance abuse program monitoring patients in transition from inpatient to outpatient care. Supervised staff and developed treatment programs. Directed community education and outreach efforts.

References Available

Nadika Nojembe

1225 Camden Road
Columbus, Ohio 43266
(614) 555-8316

Background

Dedicated, experienced RN seeking supervisory nursing position that uses my clinical, organizational, and human relations skills.

Previous Employment

November 2002 - Present
Covington General Hospital, Columbus, Ohio
Level IV Staff RN
Intensive Care Unit Supervisor

Charge nurse for 10-bed ICU. Supervise RNs, LPNs, and therapists. Facilitate implementation of multidisciplinary care plans. Schedule, train, and evaluate nursing staff. Carry out day-to-day directives of hospital administration.

April 1998 - November 2002
Good Shepherd Hospital, Milwaukee, Wisconsin
Level III Staff RN
Medical/Surgical Nurse

Observed, charted, and monitored patients' conditions. Assisted MDs with assessment and treatment. Provided general pre- and postoperative care. Developed discharge plans and instructed patients in home care.

Page 1 of 2

Previous Employment (continued)

May 1996 - April 1998
Lincoln Medical Center, Milwaukee, Wisconsin
Staff RN

Provided general nursing care at walk-in clinic, including community referral services, mental health and substance abuse interventions, and well-baby care. Instructed patients in home care and preventive health measures.

Credentials

University of Wisconsin, B.S.N., 1996
Licensed in Wisconsin (394-362392) and Ohio
(775-760381)
Member, American Nurses Association

References

A list of references will be provided on request.

JOHN B. STEVENSON

2529 Endar Road • Cleveland, Ohio 44106
(216) 555-1197 Home • (216) 555-8091 Cellular

Background

Talented nurse experienced in the areas of home health, oncology, acute coronary care, and hospice care seeks challenging full-time nursing position with successful home health agency.

Work History

HTL Home Health Ltd.
Oncology Nurse
2005 - Present

Work in conjunction with physicians, social workers, therapists, and attendants to provide complete home care for oncology patients. Administer home treatments, including chemotherapy, IV antibiotic therapy, and IV pain management. Monitor and chart patients' progress. Develop ongoing care plans. Facilitate transitions to and from hospital care.

William and Mary Medical Center
Level II CCU Nurse
2002 - 2005

Provided primary care to cardiac patients in 15-bed coronary care unit. Identified cardiac rhythms. Monitored cardiac rehabilitation. Assisted with outpatient pulmonary/cardiac rehabilitation.

Work History (continued)

Green Mountain Hospice
Intake Coordinator
1998 - 2002

Handled admissions for hospice program serving up to 20 clients per year. Cooperated with hospital and nursing home staff to arrange transition into hospice program. Explained hospice philosophy and services to clients and their families. Assisted families in seeking financial assistance and community services.

Credentials

B.S.N., Case Western Reserve, 1998
ACLS and CPR Certified

Publications

• "Dying at Home: Home Health Options for the Terminally Ill," *American Journal of Nursing*, July 2004

• "Today's Hospice," *Hospice News*, May 2002

References

Available on request

Theresa Foster

916 South Wilkins Avenue   Home: (617) 555-6879
Reynoldsburg, Ohio 43068   Pager: (617) 555-6655

Goal

A registered nurse position in the community mental health field

Overview

- Experience in community mental health nursing and counseling
- B.S.N., M.S.N. in progress
- Extensive experience with pediatric and adolescent psychiatric cases
- Strong clinical assessment skills
- In-patient and out-patient experience
- Spearheaded safety protocols
- Received consistent excellent performance reviews

Experience

Glenview Hospital
Mental Health Nurse
September 2005 to Present

Northwest Community Mental Health Center
Outpatient Mental Health Counselor
July 2001 to September 2005

Education

Ohio Nursing License #583-126052
RN, St. Catherine's School of Nursing, 2005
B.A., Psychology, Ohio State, 2001

References

Personal and professional references on request

Shane Fitzgerald, RN, M.S.N.

216 Wentworth Road
Boston, MA 02116
617-555-1050
E-mail: shanefitz2@xxx.com

Experience

- Master's prepared nurse with specialization in pediatric nursing
- Five years of experience in neonatal ICU unit at level II trauma center
- Published author with research experience
- PALS certification

Employers

Christian Children's Medical Center, Boston, MA
Level II Pediatric Staff Nurse   1/05 to Present

St. Martin's Hospital, Boston, MA
Level II Pediatric Staff Nurse   2/02 to 1/05

Liberty Hospital, Denver, CO
Level II Pediatric Staff Nurse   6/99 to 2/02

Credentials

Active RN licenses in Colorado (914-523256) and Massachusetts
   (907-441873)
M.S.N., Newberry School of Nursing, 2004
B.S.N., Amherst University, 1999
Pediatric Advanced Life Support Certification

Research/Publications

- "Pediatric Hyponatremic Seizures: New Medication Strategies," research paper presented to American Association of Pediatric Nurses, Spring 2005 Convention.
- "Pediatric Resuscitation Carts in the Neonatal ICU," *Emergency Nursing Bulletin*, January 2004, pp. 29–31.

References Available Upon Request

Mai Ling, RN

8976 Sierra Road
Newport News, Virginia 23606
Home: (804) 555-5958
Pager: (804) 555-7775

SKILLS

- Specialized trauma nursing

- General medical/surgical nursing

- Orientation of new staff

- Creation and presentation of in-house continuing education and certification programs

- Community referral

- Knowledge of computer database programs currently being implemented in local hospitals

CREDENTIALS

B.S.N. from University of Virginia, 2000; graduated with honors; financed 80 percent of tuition by working full-time while carrying full course load

Certifications: CPR, ACLS, TNS, CEN, MICN

CREDENTIALS (continued)

Virginia State Nursing License #325-595848

Memberships: American Nurses Association, Emergency Nurses Association

EMPLOYERS

St. Catherine's Hospital   Level III ER Nurse
2006 - Present

Drexler Memorial Hospital   Level II ER Nurse
2002 - 2006

Drexler Memorial Hospital   Level II Medical/Surgical Nurse
2000 - 2002

References Available

Kerry R. Babler

4665 N. Jefferson Street, #23
Chicago, IL 60640
(773) 555-6655
kbabler@xxx.com

OBJECTIVE

To provide high-quality, direct patient care with an eye toward obtaining RN licensure.

EXPERIENCE

Patient Care Technician—1/2005 to Present
Northwestern Memorial Hospital, Chicago, IL
Assist patients with activities of daily living. Obtain vital signs, record intakes and outputs, test blood glucose, perform ECGs and peripheral blood draws, and collect various specimens and lab tests. Assist RNs with procedures, including dressing changes and patient transfers.

Customer Service Shift Manager—6/2003 to 6/2004
Gold's Gym, Bloomington, IL
Responsibilities included fielding customer phone calls, addressing concerns, collecting account payments, and conducting sales transactions. Additional duties included making daily deposits, controlling inventory, and delegating work to employees.

EXPERIENCE (continued)

Certified Nursing Assistant—12/2002 to 3/2003
Manor Care Health Services, Normal, IL
Assisted residents with activities of daily living, including dressing, bathing, grooming, feeding, and transport. Took vital signs. Conducted range of motion and memory exercises for those with dementia and Alzheimer's.

Nursing Technician/Unit Secretary—7/2001 to 12/2002
BroMenn Healthcare, Normal, IL
Transcribed and processed admission paperwork, doctors' orders, and medication lists. Served as point person for unit by fielding incoming and patient calls. Nursing Technician duties included taking vital signs, assisting nurses in processing new admissions, activities of daily living, and patient glucose testing.

EDUCATION

Associate Degree of Science—2004
Heartland Community College, Normal, IL

CERTIFICATION

- CPR/AED/First Aid Certified—2005
- Specialized Dementia/Alzheimer's Training—2003
- Certified Nursing Assistant—2002
- Certified Glucose Testing Training—2002

REFERENCES AVAILABLE

· ·

Jennifer McSweeney

418 North Third Street
St. Louis, MO 63146
314-555-3626
E-mail: jmsweet35@xxx.com

· · · · · · **Goal:**

Labor and delivery staff RN position

· · · · · · **Credentials:**

B.S.N., Avila College, Kansas City, 2003
        Missouri Nursing License #975-987436
        CPR and PALS certification
        Member, Missouri Nurses Association

· · · · · · **Experience:**

2003 to Present
        Labor and Delivery Staff Nurse
        Stevenson Women's Hospital

• Evaluate and triage patients upon admission.

• Monitor patients' progress and assist them with pain
management techniques.

Page 1 of 2

• • • • • • **Experience** (continued):

• Assist physicians with delivery.

• Care for healthy newborns in nursery.

• Instruct patients in breast-feeding and infant care techniques.

• Arrange discharge planning.

• • • • • • **References:**

Available on request

Chapter 6

Sample Cover Letters

This chapter contains sample cover letters for people pursuing a wide variety of jobs and careers in nursing or who already have experience in the field.

There are many different styles of cover letters in terms of layout, level of formality, and presentation of information. These samples also represent people with varying amounts of education and work experience. Choose one cover letter or borrow elements from several different cover letters to help you construct your own.

HUMAN RESOURCES COORDINATOR
Mercy Hospital
2332 N. Lakeshore Drive
Port Huron, MI 48060

October 11, 20—

To Whom It May Concern:

I am writing to express my interest in an oncology position on 15E. I have recently completed my role transition internship on 15E—an amazing learning experience—and I am nearing graduation from my nursing program in December. I would greatly appreciate the opportunity to work with Mary McPharland and her staff again, this time as a registered nurse.

I am a fast learner, I possess a strong work ethic, and I feel completely comfortable working in a fast-paced environment and with new technologies. As I near completion of my studies in St. Clair County Community College's nursing program, I am becoming more and more enthusiastic about embarking upon my career in nursing. I know that I will make a positive contribution to Mercy's healthcare team.

I look forward to hearing from you at your convenience!

With all best wishes,

Julie Lubzik
5235 15th Avenue
Port Huron, MI 48060
810-555-9887
jlubzik@xxx.com

Mr. Jeffrey Christensen
Human Resources Director
Alzheimer's Task Force
411 Kearney Road
McLean, VA 22101

May 22, 20—

Dear Mr. Christensen:

It is rare to find a professional opportunity that allows one to dedicate time to a cause that has great personal meaning. For me, serving as the educational director for the Alzheimer's Task Force would be both professionally and personally rewarding. My background in health care education qualifies me for the job, and dealing with Alzheimer's in my own family has given me a special understanding of the challenges caregivers face.

The enclosed resume provides the details of my work history. I am fortunate to have had a wide variety of experience as a health care educator. As a result, my communications skills are strong. My writing, public relations, and media relations abilities would serve me well in developing the media campaign and educational materials you require.

Please let me know if you need further information in order to consider me for this opening.

I would enjoy meeting you in person to discuss how we might join forces to battle Alzheimer's disease.

Sincerely,

Sara Ferguson
1811 Foley Street #602
Washington, DC 20024
(202) 555-4113
E-mail: sferguson@xxx.com

Mai Ling, RN

8976 Sierra Road
Newport News, Virginia 23606
Home: (804) 555-5958
Pager: (804) 555-7775

TO: Ms. Anna Rodriguez
        Director of Nursing
        New Haven General Hospital
        876 Brookside Drive
        New Haven, Connecticut 06510

DATE: May 17, 20—

RE: *Application for Emergency Nursing Position*

Our conversation this morning regarding the new emergency department at New Haven General was most enjoyable and informative. It is heartening to know that in this era of downsizing some health care institutions are still managing to thrive. With the extra space, equipment, and staff, New Haven General will be able to do an even better job of serving the New Haven community.

I am excited at the prospect of becoming part of this growth and glad to hear that there may be room for me on New Haven's ER staff. Following is my resume, which explains in more detail my experience, which we touched on over the phone. If any other questions should arise before our meeting on May 29, please feel free to call me at (804) 555-5958. I will be at home during the next few weeks, helping my family prepare for the move to Connecticut.

In the meantime, please contact my references, two of my former supervisors: Judith Shaw at St. Catherine's, (804) 555-6978, and Warren Peterson at Drexler Memorial, (804) 555-3958. They can provide you with testimonies regarding my work ethic and the quality of care I'm able to provide in a fast-paced and lively environment like the ER.

I appreciate your taking the time to review my credentials and look forward to meeting you on the 29th!

Sincerely,

Mai Ling

Ms. Elizabeth Warren, President
Professional Nurses of New England
418 Valley View Road
Rockville, MD 20849

June 24, 20—

Dear Ms. Warren:

I was excited to learn of your current search for a successor because I believe I am uniquely qualified to continue your fine record of service to the nursing community in New England. As the enclosed resume indicates, I have an M.S.N., NLRB certification, and previous experience as a labor relations specialist and president of my state nursing organization. I'm sure you will agree that this diverse job experience, including leadership positions, would enable me to succeed in a number of key areas, including:

* Contract Negotiations
* Membership Recruitment
* Direction of Educational Efforts
* Supervision of Publishing Projects

I understand that your search for applicants will continue through the end of the month. I hope to hear from you after you have completed the arduous task of screening candidates. Should you wish to interview me at that point, I would be pleased to travel to Rockville at your convenience.

I appreciate your serious consideration of my qualifications and wish you good luck in your search for a new president.

Sincerely,

Madison Browne

Madison Browne
418 Bradley Street • Bay City, MI 48706
517-555-5967 • madisonbrowne@xxx.com

Mr. James Jackson, Director
Jackson Park School of Nursing
1349 Greenville Road
Chicago, IL 60690

November 3, 20—

Dear Mr. Jackson:

As I was reading this month's issue of the *American Journal of Nursing*, I spotted your advertisement for nursing faculty. I am enclosing my resume and a list of references so that you may consider me for the available position.

I have been a nurse educator for nearly a decade, as outlined in my resume. My experience encompasses instruction both in classroom and clinical settings, clinical nursing practice and supervision, and research. Furthermore, various aspects of my professional background uniquely qualify me for this position, including:

• Extensive clinical experience—from oncology and medical-surgical nursing to orthopedic and gerontological nursing practice

• Strong research skills, as evidenced by my receipt of a research grant from the American Nurses Foundation and publication in the *American Journal of Clinical Oncology*

• Effective teaching skills developed through instruction of students, staff, and patients in university, hospital, and outpatient clinic settings

• Proficient computer skills that include Microsoft Office and Powerchart

I am confident that my skills would enhance the faculty of Jackson Park, and I look forward to speaking with you in person.

Thank you for your consideration.

Sincerely,

Kevin Riley

622 Robinson Road
Des Plaines, IL 60016
(847) 555-6123 Home
(847) 555-8127 Work
E-mail: kriley@xxx.com

SUSAN WRIGHT

1411 Harrod Lane
Boulder, CO 80304
Home: 303-555-4958
Pager: 303-555-6789
E-mail: suewright@xxx.com

November 3, 20—

Dr. Stacy Fitzpatrik, Director
Mercy Hospice
654 Winston Court
Boulder, CO 80304

Dear Dr. Fitzpatrik:

I am writing to request that you formally consider me for the entry-level RN position that just became available at Mercy Hospice.

As you know, I have worked at Mercy for the past year as a volunteer nursing assistant. I would like to continue my tenure at Mercy as a full-time staff member after graduating from nursing school next month.

I have enclosed my resume for your review. My direct supervisor, Carol Robinson, Nurse Manager on 6 South Atrium, knows of my interest in the current nursing opening and is willing to discuss my credentials with you.

Thank you for your consideration. I sincerely hope that I can continue my successful association with Mercy this summer as your new staff RN.

All best wishes,

Susan Wright

JOHN B. STEVENSON

2529 Endar Road • Cleveland, Ohio 44106
(216) 555-1197 Home • (216) 555-8091 Cellular

Forum Home Health Care
348 Bennet Road
Cleveland, Ohio 44106
ATTN: Rosemary Best, Human Resources Specialist

August 12, 20—

Dear Ms. Best:

Like so many other nurses seeking greater autonomy and more meaningful
relationships with clients, I've shifted from hospital nursing to home health
care. For me, home health provides the best means to offer patients
professional, compassionate, holistic care. I know that Forum Home Health
Care shares these values. Several nursing colleagues, including Amanda
Preston and Elizabeth Walsh, have shared with me their positive work
experiences with your agency.

I am writing to introduce myself on the chance that you may have room for
me on your staff. I am an experienced nurse whose background includes home
health oncology nursing and hospice care. The enclosed resume provides
amplification, and both Ms. Preston and Ms. Walsh are familiar with my work
should you need personal testimonies. In addition, I would be happy to
provide you with references from several past supervisors.

Thank you for taking the time to consider my credentials. I look forward to
the possibility of working with you at Forum.

Sincerely,

John B. Stevenson, RN

VIA FAX

TO: Human Resources

FR: Miko Maramoto

RE: Patient Care Technician Position

January 17, 20—

To Whom It May Concern:

I am writing to you today to express my interest in the patient care technician position available on the labor and delivery floor at Jones Medical Center. Last fall and this spring, I completed my medical-surgical clinical rotation on 13E and my advanced physical assessment rotation on 16W at Jones. Since that time, I have completed my pediatric clinical rotation at Children's Memorial Hospital and am finishing my OB rotation at St. Joseph's.

I had amazing learning experiences at Jones and would greatly appreciate the opportunity to work with the staff again. I am available for any shift and any number of hours throughout the summer and, on a more limited basis, in the fall.

I look forward to hearing from you about how I can contribute to the outstanding care Jones is known for.

Sincerely,

Miko Maramoto
Student Nurse
2662 Charleston Way
Pittsburgh, PA 15221
412-555-6453
mmaramoto@xxx.com

JULIA SILVERMAN

453 Pratt Lane
Atlanta, Georgia 30301
(404) 555-3130
Pager: (404) 555-5674
juliesil@xxx.com

June 16, 20—

Ms. Susan Parker
Director of Nursing
McKeon Memorial Hospital
912 Central Street
Charlotte, North Carolina 28210

Dear Ms. Parker:

I enjoyed our conversation at last week's meeting of the American Psychiatric Nurses Association, and I would appreciate the opportunity to talk to you further about nursing positions at McKeon Memorial.

As you know, I currently work at Atlanta General as a level II psychiatric nurse. I have also worked in a residential substance abuse treatment center and an outpatient community mental health center. The enclosed resume sketches out my work history in greater detail.

Your research into adolescent substance abuse treatment intrigues me and is just one of the many reasons that I'm interested in working with you. Please let me know if there is any way I can contribute to the health care team at McKeon.

Cordially,

Julia Silverman

Sophie Bowman
1910 Hardy Street
Honolulu, Hawaii 96814
Home: 808-555-6668
Work: 808-555-9112
E-mail: sbowman@xxx.com

September 13, 20—

Kirk Tanaka, Director
Children's Health Foundation
2719 Hamilton Street
Honolulu, Hawaii 96814

Dear Mr. Tanaka:

I have tremendous admiration for the work your organization is doing in bringing health care to underprivileged children. Nothing would please me more than contributing to that effort by joining your staff as the assistant director. I feel well qualified for the position, having extensive nursing and health care program management experience, including my most recent work experience for Bright Horizons, a smaller community program serving underprivileged single mothers.

Please review the enclosed resume and let me know if you need any other information to consider me for the assistant director position. I would also appreciate an interview if you feel my credentials warrant serious consideration. You may reach me at home on Tuesday and Thursday (555-6668) or at work on Monday, Wednesday, and Friday (555-9112).

I feel confident that I would make an excellent addition to your staff and look forward to the opportunity of working with you at the Children's Health Foundation.

Sincerely,

Sophie Bowman

GEORGIA BETTS

1037 West Robin Road
Austin, TX 78768
(512) 555-8718
gbetts@xxx.com

May 8, 20—

Ms. Mary Fajardo
Director of Nursing
Culverton General Hospital
1402 Larson Road
Culverton, VA 12245

Dear Ms. Fajardo:

I enjoyed talking to you this morning regarding nursing opportunities at Culverton General and appreciate being able to interview with you during my visit on the 20th of this month. As a Virginia native, I am well aware of Culverton's excellent reputation in the community and would be pleased to be associated with the hospital. Your current opening in the emergency department seems especially well suited to someone with my skills, as you can see from the enclosed resume.

I have been an ER nurse since 2002 and enjoy the challenge of working in emergency medicine. My current position at St. Joseph's Hospital, a level III trauma center, has provided me with a wide range of trauma nursing experience. In addition to my on-the-job training, I have pursued extensive continuing education credits by attending in-service programs and attaining several specialized certifications such as TNS and CEN.

Of course, these details tell only part of the story. My strongest assets as a nurse are my rapport with patients and their families and my professionalism in working as a member of a team. I hope to put these qualities to work for you at Culverton General.

If any questions arise before the 20th, I am available before 3 P.M. at (512) 555-8718. I look forward to meeting you.

Sincerely,

Georgia Betts, RN, TNS, CEN

Karen Greenberg

486 Kramer Road, Uniondale, PA 18711

Home: (717) 555-8102   Cell: (717) 555-9988   E-mail: kgreen@xxx.com

October 14, 20—

Ms. Zoe Navarro
Director of Personnel
St. Vincent's Hospital
620 Riverview Drive
Gradyville, PA 19039

Dear Ms. Navarro:

A colleague of mine at Hewlett Rehabilitation Center in Uniondale, Carlos Gestoso, suggested that I write to you regarding job opportunities at St. Vincent's. As you probably know, Hewlett is closing its doors at the end of this calendar year, so I am seeking new professional opportunities.

Are you in need of an experienced RN with proven skills in educational development, quality control, and research? If so, my resume should interest you. I have served as the staff educator at Hewlett since 2003. My previous experience also includes staff nursing in a variety of medical-surgical departments.

I will call early next week to see whether you would like to arrange an interview. In the meantime, you may reach me at work, (717) 555-9878, from 9 A.M. to 5 P.M. My home phone is (717) 555-8102, and you can also reach me via cell phone at (717) 555-9988.

Thanks for considering my credentials, and I look forward to working with you in the future!

Sincerely,

Karen Greenberg

Ms. Melissa Wright
Herrington Home Health Care
1411 Grant Street
Denver, Colorado 80209

March 2, 20—

Dear Ms. Wright:

It was with great interest that I learned of your need for an intake counselor. I have been watching for such an opening at a home health agency, and I would like to apply for the position.

I have extensive nursing experience, as outlined in the enclosed resume. My background encompasses a wide cross section of medical specialties and a number of skills that would transfer well to the position of intake counselor:

• Recording patient histories
• Providing referral services
• Developing discharge plans
• Implementing cost containment procedures
• Proficiency in MS Office software, as well as Lotus Notes and
  Meeting Maker

I am confident that my abilities match your current requirements. May I call next week to arrange an interview so that we can discuss how I could contribute to your health care team?

Sincerely,

Sue Chang
245 Bishop Street
Boulder, Colorado 80209
303-555-1936
suechang@xxx.com

JESSICA STILSON, RN

411 HIGHLAND COURT

BROOKINGS, SD 57007

HOME: (605) 555-3889

CELL: (605) 555-9866

May 24, 20—

Ms. Ann Nguyen, Director of Personnel
Harrison Medical Center
7245 S. Campbell Street
Madison, WI 53792

Dear Ms. Nguyen:

As nursing becomes increasingly challenging and high-tech, health care providers are demanding the most qualified personnel possible. Harrison Medical Center is no exception, as your recent ad for a clinical transplant coordinator indicates. I feel confident that I could meet the high standards you set for your nursing staff, and I would enjoy the challenge of managing the daily operation of your transplant program.

My qualifications for the position are explained in detail in the enclosed resume. The highlights are as follows:

• Successfully manage corneal transplant program at the South Dakota State University Eye Clinic. Number of donors has increased by 20 percent during my tenure.
• Additional transplant work as certified Trauma Nurse Specialist with more than four years of experience in a level III trauma hospital emergency room.
• B.S.N. degree from South Dakota State University.
• Extensive database management, which assists in tracking donors and reduces paperwork.

I am willing to relocate and am eligible for RN licensure in the state of Wisconsin.

Please let me know if you need further information to evaluate my credentials. I look forward to discussing how I might contribute to the future success of Harrison's Clinical Transplant Program.

Cordially,

Jessica Stilson, RN

TO: Jolie Brown, Director
             Whitfield Women's Clinic
             411 Robinson Street
             Park Ridge, IL 60068

FROM: Ellen McShane
            724 Olympia Drive
            Des Moines, IA 50265

DATE: May 17, 20—

RE: Application for Charge Nurse Position

Dear Ms. Brown:

I enjoyed meeting you at the Women's Health Fair at Columbia College last weekend, and I am most interested in the charge nurse position you mentioned.

Here is the resume you requested, which details my nursing and educational background. Community health nursing is familiar territory for me, as you can see. My commitment to women's health care has also been a priority, which is why I have volunteered for Planned Parenthood for the past seven years.

I think my skills are a good match for the charge nurse position and hope that you agree. You can reach me at home at (319) 555-1284 or on my pager at (319) 555-6744 to arrange an interview. I'm enthusiastic about the possibility of working for you at Whitfield Women's Clinic and appreciate your interest.

Best wishes,

Ellen McShane

✜ MARILYN SMITH

418 Whitesburg Street
Wauconda, IL 60084
847-555-9822
marilyn_smith@xxx.com

Mr. John P. Bowen
Alexandria General Hospital
1619 Farragut Avenue
Chicago, IL 60645

December 10, 20—

Dear Mr. Bowen:

Is your organization currently in need of nursing support? If so, I am an ideal candidate for you. I have seven years of experience providing quality care to a variety of patients—from children to elders. I've been consistently praised for my performance by supervisors who tell me they value the skill and dedication I bring to my job as a nursing assistant. In addition, patients frequently express appreciation for the way in which I care for their emotional and physical needs.

I will be relocating to Chicago next month, and I would welcome the opportunity to join the team at Alexandria General. I have enclosed a resume for your review, and I would appreciate hearing from you about any available openings. I am available during the day at 847-555-9822 or via e-mail at marilyn_smith@xxx.com.

I will follow up this query letter with a phone call at the end of next week.

Thank you,

Marilyn Smith

··

ROBERT K. WARREN
121 Waverly Place
Boston, MA 02129

May 15, 20—

Ms. Georgia Pellum
Nursing Supervisor
Kingston Memorial Hospital
2602 Barrington Road
Boston, MA 02129

Dear Ms. Pellum:

I submit the enclosed resume in response to your advertised appeal for
a level II general surgical RN. Please note that my nursing background
exactly matches your current needs. With more than five years of
successful service in hospital surgical nursing, I would bring a wealth
of experience to Kingston Memorial.

My long-term career goal is to gain supervisory experience, and I have
already demonstrated leadership ability by organizing numerous in-
service programs for my current employer, Boston General. Robin
White, my current supervisor, has indicated her willingness to act as a
reference. Please feel free to contact her at 555-8311, extension 216.

It is easiest to reach me at home at 555-2716, after 3 P.M.

Thank you for your consideration. I look forward to hearing from you.

Yours truly,

Robert K. Warren

BARBARA KLINETOP
St. Xavier's Memorial Hospital
3626 North Lincoln Avenue
Chicago, IL 60613

May 11, 20—

Dear Ms. Klinetop:

I am a second-year graduate student in DePaul University's Master's Entry to Nursing Practice program, and I am very interested in becoming a nursing assistant for St. Xavier's Memorial Hospital. I have completed my medical-surgical clinical rotation and my advanced physical assessment rotation, in addition to fundamentals and psychiatric and pediatric nursing courses. I prefer to work in the float pool or on a med-surg floor but am amenable to your needs.

I learn quickly, possess a strong work ethic, and feel incredibly enthusiastic about embarking upon my career in the field of nursing. I know that I will make a positive contribution to St. Xavier's healthcare team. I am fully available to work throughout the summer and, on a more limited basis, in the fall.

I look forward to hearing from you at your convenience!

With all best wishes,

STACY GERALDI
Graduate Student Nurse

3228 North Clark Street, #64
Chicago, IL 60657
773-555-0697
stacygeraldi.com

Marguerite Kusaka

3984 Briar Street
Oakland, California 94609
Home: (414) 555-2837
Cell: (414) 555-0098
E-mail: mkusaka@xxx.com

April 17, 20—

Ms. Lucy Eisenberg, Director
Hathaway House
418 Pearson Street
Oakland, California 94609

Dear Ms. Eisenberg:

I would like your consideration for the general manager position recently advertised in the *Oakland Gazette*. The enclosed resume provides the details of my experience as a health care coordinator.

Your advertisement called for an experienced clinic director with strong financial planning and management skills, as well as extensive computer skills. As you will see, I more than meet these requirements. After researching the philosophy, mission statement, and recent positive press Hathaway House has received, I am interested in devoting myself to the day-to-day management of Hathaway House.

May I present my qualifications in person? You may reach me at (414) 555-2837 or on my cell phone at (414) 555-0098 to arrange an interview.

Cordially,

Marguerite Kusaka

JEFFREY FRANCIS

202 Bedford Lane ❖ Roselle, Illinois 60172
(630) 555-8162 Home ❖ (630) 555-3571 Cellular

June 1, 20—

Mr. Mark Martin, Director
Munroe Nursing Center
Hanover Park, Illinois 60103

Dear Mr. Martin,

I was excited to read about the position you recently advertised in the *Chicago Tribune*, which seems to match my skills exactly. I am currently responsible for the management of a midsize home health agency— Harrison Home Health. The managerial skills I have developed over the past five years at Harrison would translate well to the general manager position you're seeking to fill. Setting and managing budgets, hiring qualified personnel, matching patient's needs with staff expertise, and ensuring that Harrison Home Health is a name that is synonymous with high-quality health care are just a few of the skills I've mastered and am interested in sharing with the Munroe Nursing Center.

The enclosed resume explains my professional accomplishments in more detail. I look forward to discussing it further with you in person. I will contact you early next week to arrange an interview at your convenience. Meanwhile, thank you for your consideration.

Sincerely,

Jeff Francis

Sara McKenna
Managing Editor
Nursing News
1800 Glenwood Road
Boston, MA 02116

January 22, 20—

Dear Ms. McKenna:

As an avid reader of your magazine, I was pleased to learn of your search for a new assistant editor. My professional background includes a unique mix of editorial and nursing experience that makes me especially well qualified for the position.

I've enclosed a copy of my resume so that you may review my credentials. I also am available at your convenience for an interview. It is easiest to reach me in the mornings at work. The number there is 617-555-1202. You may also reach me by cell phone at 617-555-5546.

Beyond the skills described on my resume, I bring a high degree of dedication and dependability to my employers. I currently work part-time as the assistant educational director at Boston General. My supervisor there, Gloria Preston, is aware of my need for a full-time position and therefore supportive of my job search. You may contact her at 617-555-1204 for a reference.

Please let me know if you need any further information in order to consider me for the assistant editor position. I am sure that I would find it both personally and professionally rewarding to join the staff at *Nursing News*.

Yours truly,

Jill Schneider, RN
418 Long Street
Boston, MA 02116
617-555-5546
E-mail: jschneider@xxx.com